Important Instruction

Students, Parents, and Teachers can use the URL or QR code provided below to access two full-length Lumos GMAS practice tests. Please note that these assessments are provided in the Online format only.

URL	QR Code
Visit the URL below and place the book access code **http://www.lumoslearning.com/a/tedbooks** **Access Code: GMASMG7-58308-S**	

Lumos Learning
Developed by Expert Teachers

GMAS Online Assessments and 7th Grade Math Practice Workbook, Student Copy

Contributing Author - Aaron Spencer
Contributing Author - Nikki McGee
Executive Producer - Mukunda Krishnaswamy
Program Director - Priya L.
Designer and Illustrator - Sowmya R.

First Edition - 2020

ISBN-10: 154266666X

ISBN-13: 978-1542666664

Printed in the United States of America

For permissions and additional information contact us

Lumos Information Services, LLC
PO Box 1575, Piscataway, NJ 08855-1575
http://www.LumosLearning.com

Email: support@lumoslearning.com
Tel: (732) 384-0146
Fax: (866) 283-6471

Developed by Expert Teachers

INTRODUCTION

About Lumos tedBook for GMAS Test Practice:
This book is specifically designed to improve student achievement on the GMAS. Students perform at their best on standardized tests when they feel comfortable with the test content as well as the test format. Lumos tedBook for GMAS test ensures this with meticulously designed practice that adheres to the guidelines provided by the GMAS for the number of questions, standards, difficulty level, sessions, question types, and duration.

About Lumos Smart Test Practice:
With more than a decade of experience and expertise in developing practice resources for standardized tests, Lumos Learning has developed the most efficient methodology to help students succeed on the state assessments (See Figure 1).

Lumos Smart Test Prep Methodology offers students realistic GMAS assessment rehearsal along with providing an efficient pathway to overcome each proficiency gap.

The process starts with students taking the online diagnostic assessment. This online diagnostic test will help assess students' proficiency levels in various standards. With the completion of this diagnostic assessment, Lumos generates a personalized study plan with a standard checklist based on student performance in the online diagnostic test. Parents and educators can use this study plan to remediate the proficiency gaps with targeted standards-based practice available in the workbook.

After student completes the targeted remedial practice, they should attempt the second online GMAS practice test. Upon finishing the second assessment, Lumos will generate another individualized study plan by identifying topics that require more practice. Based on these practice suggestions, further skill building activities can be planned to help students gain comprehensive mastery needed to ensure success on the state assessment.

Lumos Smart Test Prep Methodology

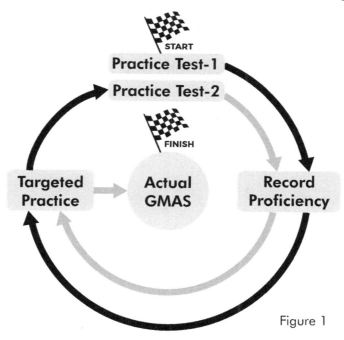

Figure 1

Table of Contents

Sign Up Online

GMAS

Grade 7 Math Practice

Unlock Digital Access

2 GMAS Practice Tests

3 Math Domains

Sign Up Now

Url: https://LumosLearning/a/tedbooks

Access Code: GMASMG7-58308-S

Access GMAS Test Practice Resources On Your Mobile Device

Online Access

for

GMAS Practice

Printed Workbook

for

Skills Practice

Download Lumos StepUp App
from Google Play Store or Apple App Store

After installing the StepUp App, scan this **QR Code** via **tedBook** section of the mobile app

Chapter 1

Lumos Smart Test Practice Methodology

Step 1: Access Online GMAS Practice Test

The online GMAS practice tests mirror the actual Georgia Milestones Assessment System (GMAS) in the number of questions, item types, test duration, test tools, and more.

After completing the test, your student will receive immediate feedback with detailed reports on standards mastery and a personalized study plan to overcome any learning gaps. With this study plan, use the next section of the workbook to practice.

Use the URL and access code provided below or scan the QR code to access the first GMAS practice test to get started.

URL	QR Code
Visit the URL below and place the book access code **http://www.lumoslearning.com/a/tedbooks** **Access Code: GMASMG7-58308-S**	

Step 2: Review the Personalized Study Plan Online

After students complete the online Practice Test 1, they can access their individualized study plan from the table of contents (Figure 2) Parents and Teachers can also review the study plan through their Lumos account (parent or teacher) portal.

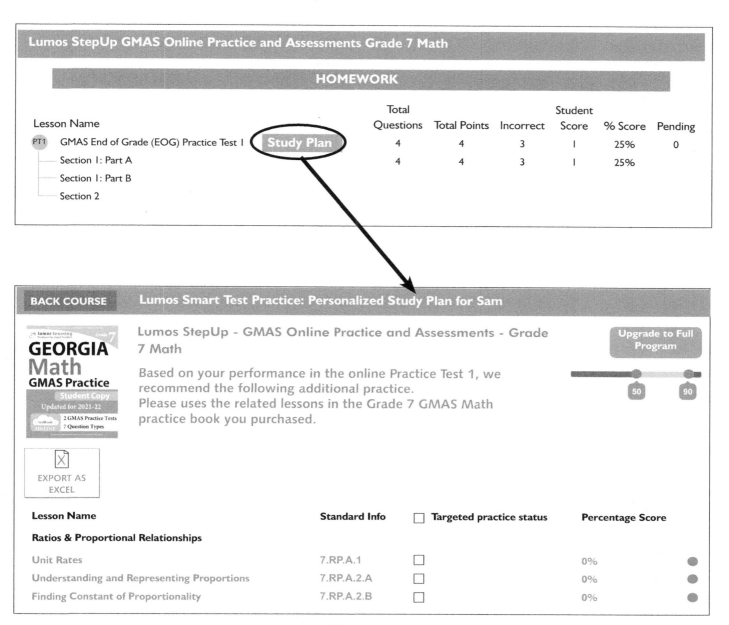

Figure 2

Step 3: Complete Targeted Practice

Using the information provided in the study plan report, complete the targeted practice using the appropriate lessons to overcome proficiency gaps. With lesson names included in the study plan, find the appropriate topics in this workbook and answer the questions provided. Marking the completed lessons in the study plan after each practice session is recommended. (See Figure 3)

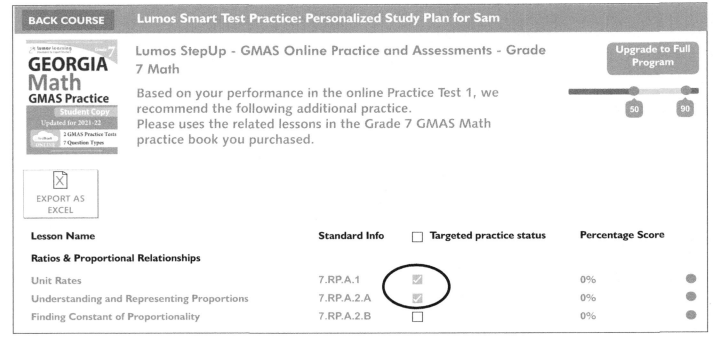

Figure 3

Step 4: Access the Practice Test 2 Online

After completing the targeted practice in this workbook, students should attempt the second GMAS practice test online. Using the student login name and password, login to the Lumos website to complete the second practice test.

Step 5: Repeat Targeted Practice

Repeat the targeted practice as per Step 3 using the second study plan report for Practice test 2 after completion of the second GMAS rehearsal.

Visit http://www.lumoslearning.com/a/lstp for more information on Lumos Smart Test Prep Methodology or Scan the QR Code

Test Taking Tips

1) **The day before the test,** make sure you get a good night's sleep.

2) **On the day of the test,** be sure to eat a good hearty breakfast! Also, be sure to arrive at school on time.

3) **During the test:**

- **Read each question carefully.**

    - Do not spend too much time on any one question. Work steadily through all questions in the section.
    - Attempt all the questions even if you are not sure of some answers.
    - If you run into a difficult question, eliminate as many choices as you can and then pick the best one from the remaining choices. Intelligent guessing will help you increase your score.
    - Also, mark the question so that if you have extra time, you can return to it after you reach the end of the section.
    - Some questions may refer to a graph, chart, or other kind of picture. Carefully review the infographics before answering the question.
    - Be sure to include explanations for your written responses and show all work.

- **While Answering Multiple-choice (EBSR) questions.**

    - Select the bubble corresponding to your answer choice.
    - Read all of the answer choices, even if think you have found the correct answer.

- **While Answering TECR questions.**

    - Read the directions of each question. Some might ask you to drag something, others to select, and still others to highlight. Follow all instructions of the question (or questions if it is in multiple parts)

Chapter 2:
Ratios & Proportional Relationships

Lesson 1: Unit Rates

You can scan the QR code given below or use the url to access additional EdSearch resources including videos and mobile apps related to *Unit Rates*.

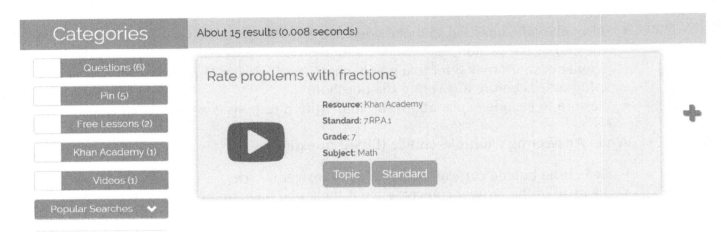

Categories	About 15 results (0.008 seconds)
Questions (6)	**Rate problems with fractions**
Pin (5)	
Free Lessons (2)	**Resource:** Khan Academy
Khan Academy (1)	**Standard:** 7.RP.A.1
Videos (1)	**Grade:** 7
Popular Searches ✔	**Subject:** Math
	Topic Standard

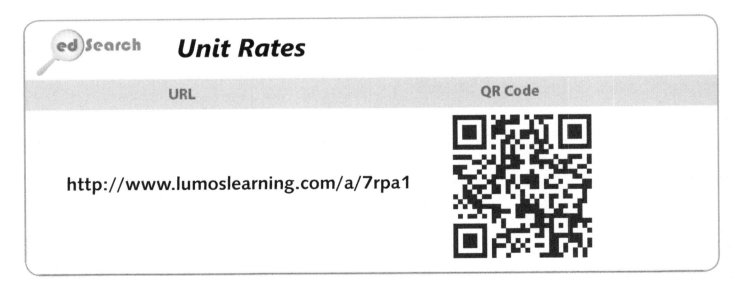

ed Search   *Unit Rates*

URL	QR Code
http://www.lumoslearning.com/a/7rpa1	

1. A tennis match was delayed because of rain. The officials were not prepared for the delay. They covered the 25ft by 20ft court with 13ft by 10ft plastic covers. How many plastic covers were needed to cover the court from the rain?

   Ⓐ 3 plastic covers
   Ⓑ 4 plastic covers
   Ⓒ 5 plastic covers
   Ⓓ 6 plastic covers

2. John eats a bowl of cereal for 3 of his 4 meals each day. He finishes two gallons of milk in eight days. How much milk does John use for one bowl of cereal? (Assume he only uses the milk for his cereal.)

   Ⓐ One-twelfth of a gallon of milk
   Ⓑ One cup of milk
   Ⓒ Two cups of milk
   Ⓓ One-sixth of a gallon of milk

3. A recipe to make a cake calls for three-fourths of a cup of milk. Mary used this cake as the first layer of a wedding cake. The second layer was half the size of the first layer, and the third layer was half the size of the second layer. How much milk would be used for the entire wedding cake?

   Ⓐ One and two-thirds cups of milk
   Ⓑ One and one-third cups of milk
   Ⓒ One and five-sixteenths cups of milk
   Ⓓ One cup of milk

4. One third of a quart of paint covers one fourth of a basketball court. How much paint does it take to paint the entire basketball court?

   Ⓐ one and one-third quarts
   Ⓑ one quart
   Ⓒ one and one-fourth quarts
   Ⓓ one and three-fourths quarts

5. The total cost of 100 pencils purchased at a constant rate is $39.00. What is the unit price?

   Ⓐ $39.00
   Ⓑ $3.90
   Ⓒ $0.39
   Ⓓ $0.039

6. A construction worker was covering the bathroom wall with tiles. He covered three-fifths of the wall with 50 tiles. How many tiles will it take to cover the entire wall?

   Ⓐ 83 tiles
   Ⓑ 83 and one-third tiles
   Ⓒ 85 tiles
   Ⓓ 83 and one-half tiles

7. Jim ran four-fifths of a mile and dropped out of the 1600 meter race. His pace was 12 miles an hour until the point he dropped out of the race. How many minutes did he run?

   Ⓐ 4 minutes and 30 seconds
   Ⓑ 4 minutes
   Ⓒ 4 minutes and 20 seconds
   Ⓓ 4 minutes and 10 seconds

8. Ping played three-fourths of a football game. The game was three and a half hours long. How many hours did Ping play in this game?

   Ⓐ 2 hours 37 minutes
   Ⓑ 2 hours 37 minutes and 30 seconds
   Ⓒ 2 hours 37 minutes and 20 seconds
   Ⓓ 2 hours 37 minutes and 10 seconds

9. Bill is working out by running up and down the steps at the local stadium. He runs a different number of steps in random order.

   Which of the following is his best time of steps per minute?

   Ⓐ 25 steps in 5 minutes
   Ⓑ 30 steps in 5.5 minutes
   Ⓒ 20 steps in 4.5 minutes
   Ⓓ 15 steps in 4 minutes

10. Doogle drove thirty and one-third miles toward his brother's house in one-third of an hour. About how long will the entire hundred mile trip take at this constant speed?

   Ⓐ 1 hour
   Ⓑ 1 hour and 6 minutes
   Ⓒ 1 hour and 1 minutes
   Ⓓ 1 hour and 3 minutes

11. **A store is selling T-Shirts. Which is the best deal? Select all correct answers that apply.**

   Ⓐ 8 for $26
   Ⓑ 5 for $30
   Ⓒ 4 for $15
   Ⓓ 12 for $39
   Ⓔ 10 for $45

12. **Read each sentence and select whether the rate is a rate or unit rate.**

	Rate	Unit Rate
The earth rotates 1.25 degrees in 5 minutes.	○	○
Sarah reads 13 pages in 1/3 of an hour.	○	○
A man pays $45.24 for 16 gallons of gasoline.	○	○
The car drives 25 miles per hour.	○	○
The soup costs $1.23 per ounce.	○	○
40 millimeters of rain fell in 1 minute.	○	○

13. **What is the unit rate for a pound of seed? Circle the correct answer choice.**

Pounds of Seed	Total Cost
10	$17.50
20	$35.00
30	$52.50
40	$70.00

   Ⓐ $3.50
   Ⓑ $1.75
   Ⓒ $17.50
   Ⓓ $7.25

Chapter 2

Lesson 2: Understanding and Representing Proportions

You can scan the QR code given below or use the url to access additional EdSearch resources including videos and mobile apps related to *Understanding and Representing Proportions*.

ed Search *Understanding and Representing Proportions*

URL	QR Code
http://www.lumoslearning.com/a/7rpa2a	

1. The following table shows two variables in a proportional relationship:

a	b
2	6
3	9
4	12

   Which of the following is an algebraic statement showing the relationship between a and b.

   Ⓐ a = 3b
   Ⓑ b = 3a
   Ⓒ b = 1/3 (a)
   Ⓓ a = 1/2 (b)

2. If the ratio of the length of a rectangle to its width is 3 to 2, what is the length of a rectangle whose width is 4 inches?

   Ⓐ 4 in.
   Ⓑ 5 in.
   Ⓒ 6 in.
   Ⓓ 7 in.

3. The following table shows two variables in a proportional relationship:

e	f
5	25
6	30
7	35

   Using the relationship between e and f as shown in this table, find the value of f when e = 11.

   Ⓐ 40
   Ⓑ 45
   Ⓒ 50
   Ⓓ 55

4. The following table shows two variables in a proportional relationship:

c	d
4	8
5	10
6	12

If c and d are proportional, then d = kc where k is the constant of proportionality.

Which of the following represents k in this case?

- Ⓐ k = 1
- Ⓑ k = 2
- Ⓒ k = 3
- Ⓓ k = 4

5. Ricky's family wants to invite his classroom to a "get acquainted" party. If 20 students attend the party then it will cost $100. Assuming the relationship between cost and guests is proportional, which of the following will be the cost if 29 students attend?

- Ⓐ $129
- Ⓑ $135
- Ⓒ $139
- Ⓓ $145

6. Which of the following pairs of ratios form a proportion?

- Ⓐ 9 boys to 5 girls and 12 boys to 8 girls
- Ⓑ 9 boys to 5 girls and 18 boys to 10 girls
- Ⓒ 9 boys to 5 girls and 13 boys to 9 girls
- Ⓓ 9 boys to 5 girls and 27 boys to 14 girls

7. If the local supermarket is selling oranges for *p* cents each and Mrs. Jones buys *n* oranges, write an equation for the total *(t)*, that Mrs. Jones pays for oranges.

- Ⓐ t = p + n
- Ⓑ t = p - n
- Ⓒ t = pn
- Ⓓ t = p/n

8. The ratio of Kathy's earnings to her hours worked is constant. This fact implies which of the following?

  Ⓐ Kathy's earnings are proportional to her hours of work.
  Ⓑ If Kathy works harder during her 8 hours of work today, her income for today will be greater than if she just takes it easy.
  Ⓒ If Kathy only works a half day today, her earnings will be the same as if she worked all day.
  Ⓓ If Kathy takes an extra hour for lunch, it will not affect her earnings for the day.

9. Write a mathematical statement (equation) for the relationship between feet and yards.

  Ⓐ number of feet / number of yards = 3
  Ⓑ number of yards / number of feet = 3
  Ⓒ number of feet - number of yards = 3
  Ⓓ number of feet + number of yards = 3

10. The ratio of the measurement of a length in yards to the measurement of the same length in feet is a constant. This implies that __?

  Ⓐ the measurement of a length in yards is directly proportional to the measurement of the same length in feet.
  Ⓑ the measurement in yards of a length is inversely proportional to the measurement of the same length in feet.
  Ⓒ the measurement in yards of a length is equivalent to the measurement of the same length in feet.
  Ⓓ There is no relationship between the two measurements.

11. Look at the table below. Decide whether the table shows a proportional relationship between x and y. Write Yes if the relationship is proportional or write No if the relationship is not proportional in the box given below.

x	2	4	7	10
y	4	16	49	100

12. Suppose you are buying pizzas for a party. An equation that represents the cost (y) in dollars for x number of pizzas is y=18x.

Does the equation y=18x represent a proportional relationship? Instruction : Check all that are true

Ⓐ No, the graph of the equation does not pass through the origin.
Ⓑ Yes, the graph of the equation is a straight line
Ⓒ Yes, the graph of the equation passes through the origin.
Ⓓ No, the graph of the equation is not a straight line.

13. The table shows a proportional relationship between x and y. For each value of x and y, match it to the correct unit rate $\frac{y}{x}$ in it's simplest form.

	$\frac{6}{1}$	$\frac{3}{1}$	$\frac{9}{1}$
x = 3 and y = 27	☐	☐	☐
x = 9 and y = 81	☐	☐	☐
x = 21 and y = 126	☐	☐	☐
x = 14 and y = 84	☐	☐	☐
x = 12 and y = 36	☐	☐	☐
x = 15 and y = 45	☐	☐	☐

Chapter 2

Lesson 3: Finding Constant of Proportionality

You can scan the QR code given below or use the url to access additional EdSearch resources including videos and mobile apps related to *Finding Constant of Proportionality*.

 **Finding Constant of Proportionality**

URL	QR Code
http://www.lumoslearning.com/a/7rpa2b	

1. **According to the graph, what is the constant of proportionality?**

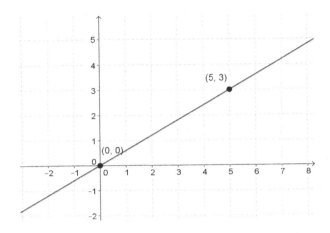

Ⓐ $\dfrac{3}{5}$

Ⓑ 5

Ⓒ 3

Ⓓ $\dfrac{1}{3}$

2. **According to the table, how much does one ticket cost?**

Number of Tickets	Total Cost
3	$ 21.00
4	$ 28.00
5	$ 35.00
6	$ 42.00

Ⓐ $21.00
Ⓑ $4.75
Ⓒ $7.00
Ⓓ $16.50

3. **If y = 3x, what is the constant of proportionality between y and x?**

   Ⓐ 1
   Ⓑ 0.30
   Ⓒ 1.50
   Ⓓ 3

4. **When Frank buys three packs of pens, he knows he has 36 pens. When he buys five packs, he knows he has 60 pens. What is the constant of proportionality between the number of packs and the number of pens?**

   Ⓐ 12
   Ⓑ 10
   Ⓒ 36
   Ⓓ 60

5. **What is the unit rate for the number of hours of study each week per class?**

   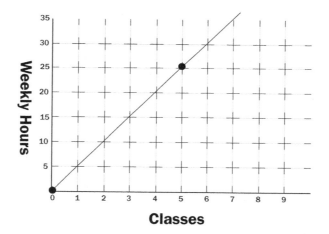

   Ⓐ 25 hours
   Ⓑ 5 hours
   Ⓒ 7 hours
   Ⓓ 10 hours

6. **What is the constant of proportionality in the following equation?**

   B = 1.25C

   Ⓐ 1.00
   Ⓑ 0.25
   Ⓒ 1.25
   Ⓓ 2.50

7. When Georgia buys 3 boxes of peaches, she has 40 pounds more than when she buys 1 box of peaches. How many pounds of peaches are in each box?

Ⓐ 40
Ⓑ 60
Ⓒ 20
Ⓓ 3

8. Look at the table below:

X	5	6	7	8
Y	90	108	126	144

What is the constant of proportionality of y to x. Enter your answer in the box given below.

9. Suppose the relationship between x and y is proportional. If the constant of proportionality of y to x is 16, select possible values for y and x.

Ⓐ x = 6 and y = 96
Ⓑ x = 96 and y = 6
Ⓒ x = 9 and y = 90
Ⓓ x = 144 and y = 9

10. In proportional relationships, there are dependent and independent variables. Match each situation to whether it is an independent variable or not.

	Independent Variable	Dependent Variable
The number of concert tickets sold is based on how many hours the ticket booth is open. What kind of variable is the number of hours the ticket booth is open?	☐	☐
The number of cans that is collected for a charity drive is based on how many students bring in cans. What kind of variable is the number of students?	☐	☐
The number of buses needed for a field trip depends on how many students are going on the field trip. What kind of variable is the number of buses?	☐	☐
The number of cell phone towers built is determined by how many customers are in the area. What kind of variable is the number of cell phone towers?	☐	☐

Chapter 2

Lesson 4: Represent Proportions by Equations

You can scan the QR code given below or use the url to access additional EdSearch resources including videos and mobile apps related to *Represent Proportions by Equations*.

 **Represent Proportions by Equations**

URL	QR Code
http://www.lumoslearning.com/a/7rpa2c	

1. 3 hats cost a total of $18. Which equation describes the total cost, C, in terms of the number of hats, n?

   Ⓐ   C = 3n
   Ⓑ   C = 6n
   Ⓒ   C = 0.5n
   Ⓓ   3C = n

2. Use the data in the table to give an equation to represent the proportional relationship.

x	y
0.5	7
1	14
1.5	21
2	28

   Ⓐ   y = 14x
   Ⓑ   y = 7x
   Ⓒ   7y = x
   Ⓓ   21y = x

3. Kelli has purchased a membership at the gym for the last four months. She has paid the same amount each month, and her total cost so far has been $100. What equation expresses the proportional relationship of the cost and month?

   Ⓐ   C = 100m
   Ⓑ   C = 50m
   Ⓒ   C = 4m
   Ⓓ   C = 25m

4. When buying bananas at the market, Marco pays $4.50 for 5 pounds. What is the relationship between pounds, p, and cost, C?

   Ⓐ   C = 4.5p
   Ⓑ   C = 5p
   Ⓒ   C = 0.9p
   Ⓓ   C = 22.5p

5. The cost to rent an apartment is proportional to the number of square feet in the apartment. An 800 square foot apartment costs $600 per month. What equation represents the relationship between area, a, and cost, C?

    Ⓐ C = 0.75a
    Ⓑ C = 1.33a
    Ⓒ C = 8a
    Ⓓ C = 6a

6. A school has to purchase new desks for their classrooms. They have to purchase 350 new desks, and they pay $7000. What equation demonstrates the relationship between the number of desks, d, and the total cost, C?

    Ⓐ C = 10d
    Ⓑ C = 20d
    Ⓒ C = 70d
    Ⓓ C = 35d

7. A soccer club is hosting a tournament with 12 teams involved. Each team has a set number of players, and there are a total of 180 players involved in the tournament. Which equation represents the proportional relationship between teams, t, and players, p?

    Ⓐ p = 15t
    Ⓑ p = 12t
    Ⓒ p = 18t
    Ⓓ p = 11t

8. A package of three rolls of tape costs $5 per pack. What is the proportional relationship between cost, C, and package of tape, p?

    Ⓐ C = 1.67p
    Ⓑ C = 15p
    Ⓒ C = 3p
    Ⓓ C = 5p

9. Freddy is building a house and has 5 loads of gravel delivered for the work. His total cost for the gravel is $1750. Which equation correctly shows the relationship between cost, C, and loads of gravel, g?

    Ⓐ C = 5g
    Ⓑ C = 350g
    Ⓒ C = 75g
    Ⓓ C = 225g

10. Use the graph to write an equation for the proportional relationship between the number of hours Corrie works, h, and her total pay, P.

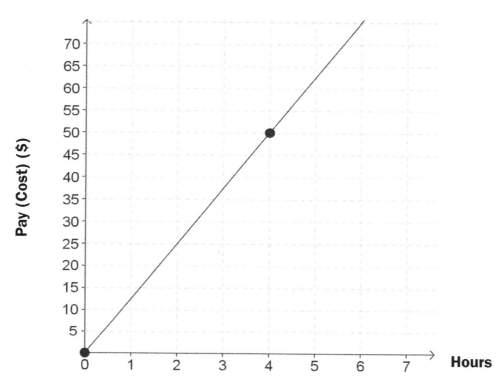

- Ⓐ P = 12.50h
- Ⓑ P = 50h
- Ⓒ P = 4h
- Ⓓ P = 22.50h

11. You run 9.1 miles in 1.3 hours at a steady rate. Write an equation that represents the proportional relationship between the x hours you run and the distance y in miles that you travel? Write the equation in the box given below

12. Sally paid $3.50 for 7 apples. Write an equation to represent the total cost y of buying x apples.

Instruction: Select the correct equation to describe the situation. There may be more than one correct answer.

(A) y = 7x
(B) 3.50y = x
(C) y = 0.50x
(D) x = 7
(E) y = 3.50x
(F) $y = \dfrac{3.50}{7}x$

13. Solve each proportion for x and match it with the correct solution for x.

	x = 9	x = 10	x = 7
$\dfrac{x}{15} = \dfrac{3}{5}$	☐	☐	☐
$\dfrac{16}{14} = \dfrac{8}{x}$	☐	☐	☐
$\dfrac{4}{20} = \dfrac{2}{x}$	☐	☐	☐
$\dfrac{75}{x} = \dfrac{50}{6}$	☐	☐	☐

Chapter 2

Lesson 5: Significance of Points on Graphs of Proportions

You can scan the QR code given below or use the url to access additional EdSearch resources including videos and mobile apps related to *Significance of Points on Graphs of Proportions.*

Significance of Points on Graphs of Proportions by Equations

URL	QR Code
http://www.lumoslearning.com/a/7rpa2d	

1. Which point on the graph of the straight line demonstrates that the line represents a proportion?

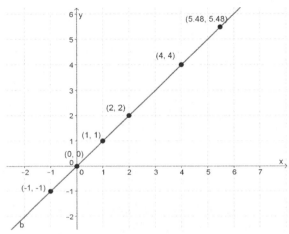

Ⓐ (2, 2)
Ⓑ (0, 0)
Ⓒ (5.48, 5.48)
Ⓓ (-1, -1)

2. Which point on the graph of the straight line names the unit rate of the proportional relationship?

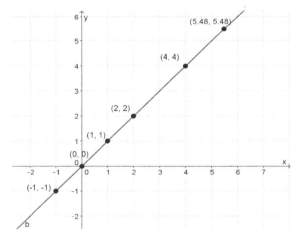

Ⓐ (1, 1)
Ⓑ (0, 0)
Ⓒ (2, 2)
Ⓓ (4, 4)

3. The graph shows the relationship between the number of classes in the school and the total number of students. How many students are there per class?

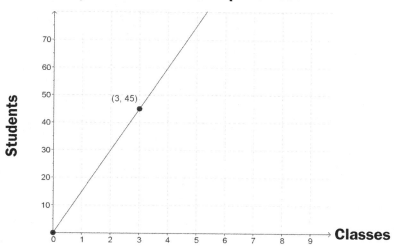

Ⓐ 45 students
Ⓑ 3 students
Ⓒ 135 students
Ⓓ 15 students

4. Use the information given on the graph to find the value of y.

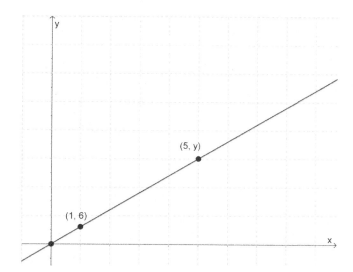

Ⓐ 30
Ⓑ 5
Ⓒ 10
Ⓓ 11

5. **In order for the relationship to be proportional, what other point must be a part of the graph?**

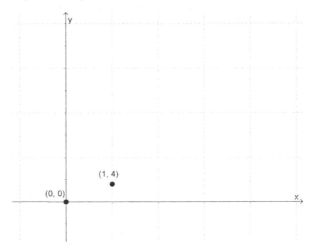

   Ⓐ (5, 10)
   Ⓑ (5, 25)
   Ⓒ (5, 15)
   Ⓓ (5, 20)

6. **What is the unit rate of Birthday presents per child?**

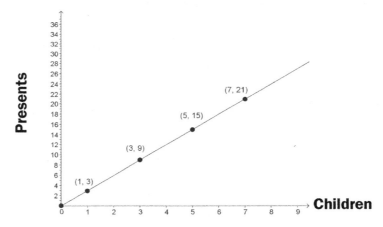

   Ⓐ 21 presents
   Ⓑ 9 presents
   Ⓒ 3 presents
   Ⓓ 15 presents

7. **What is the unit rate of bushels of apples per tree?**

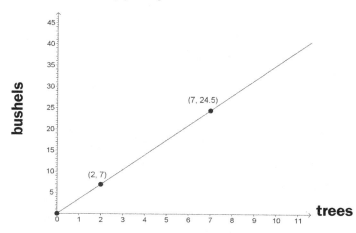

Ⓐ 3.5
Ⓑ 7
Ⓒ 24.5
Ⓓ 14

8. **Which point represents the profit if no boxes of popcorn are sold for the fundraiser?**

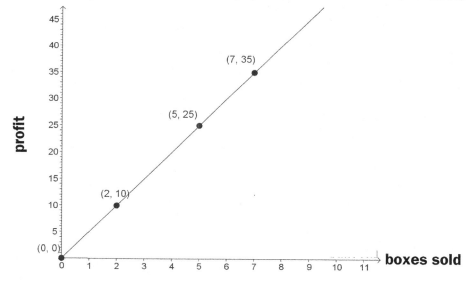

Ⓐ (5, 25)
Ⓑ (7, 35)
Ⓒ (0, 0)
Ⓓ (2, 10)

9. If the relationship between x and y is proportional, what point on the line will indicate the unit rate of that relationship?

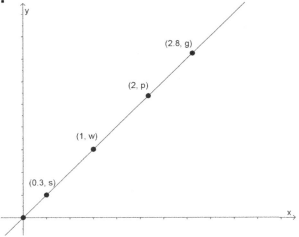

Ⓐ (2, p)
Ⓑ (0.3, s)
Ⓒ (2.8, g)
Ⓓ (1, w)

10. According to the information given on the graph, how much would 20 boards cost?

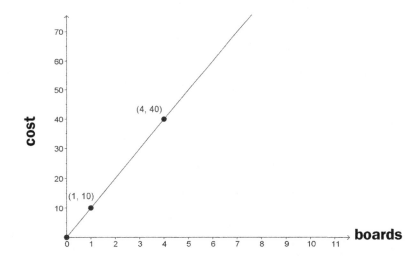

Ⓐ $200
Ⓑ $400
Ⓒ $80
Ⓓ $120

11. **Does this graph represent a proportional relationship? Enter your answer as "Yes" or "No" in the box given below.**

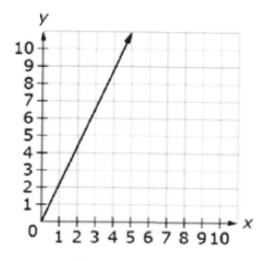

12. **What do the points on the graph mean? Select all the correct answers.**

Ⓐ After 2 weeks, you have saved $94
Ⓑ After 94 weeks, you have saved $2
Ⓒ After 10 weeks, you have saved $94
Ⓓ After 4 weeks, you have saved $188
Ⓔ After 0 weeks, you have saved $10

13. Match the situations to the corresponding graphs.

	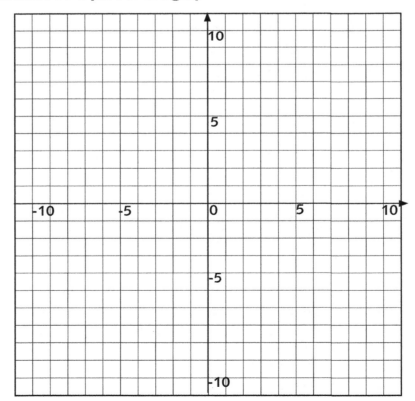	
Jake ran 3 km in 9 minutes.	◯	◯
Sara walked 3 feet in 30 seconds.	◯	◯
After 1 minute, the turtle had traveled 6 feet.	◯	◯
It took Roger 15 minutes to walk 5 km.	◯	◯

14. Plot the points (0,0) and (1,4) on the graph. In order for the relationship to be proportional, what other point must be a part of the graph

Chapter 2

Lesson 6: Applying Ratios and Percents

You can scan the QR code given below or use the url to access additional EdSearch resources including videos and mobile apps related to *Applying Ratios and Percents*.

 **Applying Ratios and Percents**

URL	QR Code
http://www.lumoslearning.com/a/7rpa3	

1. **What value of x will make these two expressions equivalent?**

    $\dfrac{-3}{7}$ and $\dfrac{x}{21}$

    Ⓐ x = -3
    Ⓑ x = 7
    Ⓒ x = 9
    Ⓓ x = -9

2. **If p varies proportionally to s, and p = 10 when s = 2, which of the following equations correctly models this relationship?**

    Ⓐ p = 5s
    Ⓑ p = 10s
    Ⓒ s = 10p
    Ⓓ 2s = 10p

3. **Solve for x, if** $\dfrac{72}{108}$ **and** $\dfrac{x}{54}$ **are equivalent.**

    Ⓐ x = 18
    Ⓑ x = 36
    Ⓒ x = 54
    Ⓓ x = 24

4. **At one particular store, the sale price, s, is always 75% of the displayed price, d. Which of the following equations correctly shows how to calculate s from d?**

    Ⓐ d = 75s
    Ⓑ s = 0.75d
    Ⓒ s = d - 0.75
    Ⓓ s = d + 75

5. **When x = 6, y = 4. If y is proportional to x, what is the value for y when x = 9?**

    Ⓐ 4

    Ⓑ $\dfrac{2}{3}$

    Ⓒ 3
    Ⓓ 6

6. Jim is shopping for a suit to wear to his friend's wedding. He finds the perfect one on sale at 30% off. If the original price was $250.00, what will the selling price be after the discount?

   Ⓐ $75
   Ⓑ $175
   Ⓒ $200
   Ⓓ $220

7. If Julie bought her prom dress on sale at 15% off and paid $110.49 before tax, find the original price of her dress.

   Ⓐ $126.55
   Ⓑ $129.99
   Ⓒ $135.00
   Ⓓ $139.99

8. A plot of land is listed for sale with the following measurements: 1300 ft x 982 ft. When the buyer measured the land, he found that it measured 1285 ft by 982 ft. What was the % of error of the area of the plot?

   Ⓐ 1.47%
   Ⓑ 14.73%
   Ⓒ 1.15%
   Ⓓ 11.7%

9. Pierre received a parking ticket whose cost is $22.00. Each month that he failed to make payment, fees of $7.00 were added. By the time he paid the ticket, his bill was $36.00. What was the ratio of fees to the cost of the ticket?

   Ⓐ $\dfrac{36}{22}$

   Ⓑ $\dfrac{22}{36}$

   Ⓒ $\dfrac{7}{22}$

   Ⓓ $\dfrac{7}{11}$

10. Sara owns a used furniture store. She bought a chest for $42 and sold it for $73.50. What percent did she mark up the chest?

   Ⓐ 100%
   Ⓑ 75%
   Ⓒ 42%
   Ⓓ 31.5%

11. What is 30% of 64? Enter your answer in the box given below.

12. Which of the expressions equals 60%? There can be more than 1 correct answer, select all the correct answers.

   Ⓐ 48 of 100
   Ⓑ 32.4 of 54
   Ⓒ 3 of 5
   Ⓓ 4 of 5
   Ⓔ 32 of 53

13. Read each of the equation and match it to whether it is part, percent or whole.

	Part	Percent	Whole
What is 35% of 15?	☐	☐	☐
4% of what number is 46?	☐	☐	☐
$y = .76 \times 43$	☐	☐	☐
$14 = m \times 56$	☐	☐	☐

End of Ratios and Proportional Relationships

Chapter 3: The Number System

Lesson 1: Rational Numbers, Addition & Subtraction

You can scan the QR code given below or use the url to access additional EdSearch resources including videos and mobile apps related to *Rational Numbers, Addition & Subtraction.*

Categories	About 195 results (0.008 seconds)
Videos (106)	(CCSS: 7.NS.A.1, 7.NS.A.2) This number sense activity bundle focuses on integer operations. Students will add, subtract, multiply and divide rationâ€¦
Khan Academy (65)	
Questions (17)	
Pin (5)	Resource: Pin
Free Lessons (2)	
Popular Searches ∨	

ed Search *Rational Numbers, Addition & Subtraction*

URL	QR Code
http://www.lumoslearning.com/a/7nsa1	

1. Evaluate: 25 + 2.005 - 7.253 - 2.977

   Ⓐ -16.775
   Ⓑ 16.775
   Ⓒ 167.75
   Ⓓ 1.6775

2. Add and/or subtract as indicated : $-3\dfrac{4}{5} + 9\dfrac{7}{10} - 2\dfrac{11}{20} =$

   Ⓐ $3\dfrac{7}{20}$

   Ⓑ $4\dfrac{7}{10}$

   Ⓒ $4\dfrac{9}{20}$

   Ⓓ $3\dfrac{1}{20}$

3. Linda and Carrie made a trip from their hometown to a city about 200 miles away to attend a friend's wedding. The following chart shows their distances, stops and times. What part of their total trip did they spend driving?

3hr	driving
15 min	rest stop
1 1/2 hr	driving
1 hr	rest stop
20 min	driving

   Ⓐ $\dfrac{4}{5}$

   Ⓑ $\dfrac{2}{5}$

   Ⓒ $\dfrac{58}{73}$

   Ⓓ $\dfrac{99}{100}$

4. If $a = \dfrac{5}{6}$, $b = -\dfrac{2}{3}$ and $c = -1\dfrac{1}{3}$, find a - b - c.

    Ⓐ $-1\dfrac{1}{6}$

    Ⓑ $2\dfrac{5}{6}$

    Ⓒ $-2\dfrac{1}{6}$

    Ⓓ $-2\dfrac{5}{6}$

5. If Ralph ate half of his candy bar followed by half of the remainder followed by half of that remainder, what part was left?

    Ⓐ $\dfrac{1}{4}$

    Ⓑ $\dfrac{1}{8}$

    Ⓒ $\dfrac{1}{6}$

    Ⓓ $\dfrac{1}{3}$

6. Mary is making a birthday cake to surprise her mom. She needs $3\dfrac{1}{2}$ cups of flour but she only has $\dfrac{1}{3}$ cup. How much more flour does she need?

7. **Ricky purchased shoes for $159.95 and then exchanged them at a buy 1, get 1 half off sale. The shoes that he purchased on his return trip were $74.99 and $68.55. How much did he receive back from the store after his second transaction?**

   A $37.50
   B $68.55
   C $34.28
   D $50.68

8. **Simplify the following expression:**

   $3.24 - 1.914 - 6.025 + 9.86 - 2.2 + 5\dfrac{1}{2} =$

   A -8.461
   B 8.461
   C -11.259
   D 11.259

9. **John had $76.00. He gave Jim $42.45 and gave Todd $21.34. John will receive $14.50 later in the evening. How much money will John have later that night?**

   A $25.71
   B $26.67
   C $26.71
   D $24.71

10. **Jeri has had a savings account since she entered first grade. Each month of the first year she saved $1.00. Each month of the second year she saved $2.00 etc until she completed ten years in which she saved $10.00 each month. How much does she have saved at the end of ten years?**

    A $660
    B $648
    C $636
    D $624

11. **Solve : $\dfrac{3}{7} + \left(-\dfrac{5}{7}\right)$ Write your answer in the box given below.**

12. Which expressions equal $-\dfrac{3}{4}$? Select all the correct answers.

Ⓐ $\dfrac{1}{8} - \dfrac{7}{8}$

Ⓑ $\dfrac{7}{8} - \dfrac{1}{8}$

Ⓒ $-\dfrac{6}{4} + \dfrac{3}{4}$

Ⓓ $\dfrac{1}{4} + \dfrac{1}{8}$

13. Read the number sentences below and match it with the correct associated property.

	Associative Property of Addition	Inverse Property of Addition	Identity Property of Addition
$\dfrac{2}{5} + 0 = \dfrac{2}{5}$	○	○	○
$\dfrac{1}{4} + \left(\dfrac{2}{3} + \dfrac{7}{8}\right) = \left(\dfrac{1}{4} + \dfrac{2}{3}\right) + \dfrac{7}{8}$	○	○	○
$\dfrac{6}{7} + -\dfrac{6}{7} = 0$	○	○	○

Chapter 3

Lesson 2: Add and Subtract Rational Numbers

You can scan the QR code given below or use the url to access additional EdSearch resources including videos and mobile apps related to *Add and Subtract Rational Numbers*.

 **Add and Subtract Rational Numbers**

URL	QR Code
http://www.lumoslearning.com/a/7nsa1b	

1. If p + q has a value that is exactly $\dfrac{1}{3}$ less than p, what is the value of q?

    (A) $\dfrac{-1}{3}$

    (B) $\dfrac{2}{5}$

    (C) $\dfrac{1}{3}$

    (D) $\dfrac{-2}{5}$

2. What is the sum of k and the opposite of k?

    (A) 2k
    (B) k + 1
    (C) 0
    (D) –1

3. If p + q has a value of $\dfrac{12}{5}$, and p has a value of $\dfrac{4}{5}$, what is the value of q?

    (A) $\dfrac{5}{8}$

    (B) $\dfrac{8}{5}$

    (C) $\dfrac{1}{3}$

    (D) $\dfrac{3}{2}$

4. What is the value of b in the diagram?

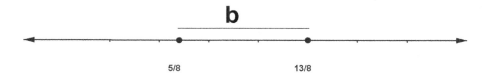

    (A) 0.8
    (B) 1
    (C) 1.8
    (D) 2.2

5. t has a value of $\dfrac{5}{2}$. p is the sum of t and v, and p has a value of 0. What is the value of v?

Ⓐ $\dfrac{-1}{3}$

Ⓑ 4

Ⓒ 2.5

Ⓓ $\dfrac{-5}{2}$

6. **What is the value of n in the diagram?**

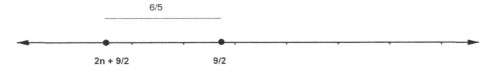

Ⓐ $\dfrac{6}{5}$

Ⓑ 0.6

Ⓒ $\dfrac{-3}{5}$

Ⓓ 2.1

7. **What is the sum of 10 and –10?**

Ⓐ 20

Ⓑ 0

Ⓒ 1

Ⓓ –20

8. **If the value of r is $\dfrac{-1}{3}$ and t has a value of $\dfrac{-1}{2}$, will t + r be to the right or left of t on a number line, and why?**

Ⓐ To the left because the absolute value of r is less than the absolute value of t.

Ⓑ To the right because the absolute value of r is less than the absolute value of t, and both numbers are negative.

Ⓒ To the left because r is a negative value being added to t.

Ⓓ To the left because the sum of two negative numbers is always negative.

9. If the value of A is 3, and the value of B is $\dfrac{-2}{3}$, how far apart will A and B be on a number line?

10. The distance between H and K on a number line is $\dfrac{9}{4}$. If K has a value of $\dfrac{7}{4}$, which of the following might be the value of H?

   Ⓐ $\dfrac{2}{4}$

   Ⓑ $\dfrac{9}{4}$

   Ⓒ - 4

   Ⓓ $\dfrac{-1}{2}$

11. Solve $\dfrac{9}{14}$ - $\dfrac{3}{14}$ and indicate it by shading the relevant boxes.

12. Enter the missing part of the addition or subtraction problem into the blanks in the table.

$-\dfrac{11}{3}$	+	$\dfrac{2}{13}$	$-\dfrac{9}{13}$
3.2		-5.7	8.9
$-2\dfrac{3}{4}$	-		4
	+	8.1	-5.1

Chapter 3

Lesson 3: Additive Inverse and Distance Between Two Points on a Number Line

You can scan the QR code given below or use the url to access additional EdSearch resources including videos and mobile apps related to *Additive Inverse and Distance Between Two Points on a Number Line.*

 Search

Additive Inverse and Distance Between Two Points on a Number Line

URL	QR Code
http://www.lumoslearning.com/a/7nsa1c	

1. **Which of the following is the same as 7 – (3 + 4)?**

    Ⓐ 7 + (−3) + (−4)
    Ⓑ 7 +(−3 + 4)
    Ⓒ 7 + 7
    Ⓓ −7 – 7

2. **Which of the following expressions represents the distance between the two points?**

    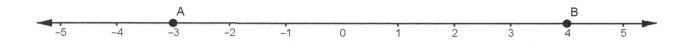

    Ⓐ | 4 - 3 |
    Ⓑ (-3) -4
    Ⓒ | (-3) - 4 |
    Ⓓ 4 - 3

3. **Kyle and Mark started at the same location. Kyle traveled 5 miles due east, while Mark traveled 3 miles due West. How far apart are they?**

    Ⓐ 2 miles
    Ⓑ 8 miles
    Ⓒ 15 miles
    Ⓓ 12 miles

4. **The distance between G and H on the number line is | 5 - (- 2) |. What might be the coordinate of H?**

    Ⓐ 2
    Ⓑ 7
    Ⓒ 6
    Ⓓ −2

5. **Which of the following is the same as 2x − 3y − z?**

Ⓐ 2x − (3y − z)
Ⓑ 2x + (−3y) − z
Ⓒ 2x + 3y − z
Ⓓ (−2x) − 3y − z

6. **If Brad lives 5 blocks north of the park and Easton lives 7 blocks south of the park, which of the following correctly represents an expression for the distance between their homes?**

Ⓐ | 5 - (-7) |
Ⓑ 7 - 5
Ⓒ 3 - (- 4)
Ⓓ | 5 + (-7) |

7. **For what numbers will the statement be true?: t − (w) = t + (−w)**

Ⓐ All positive numbers only
Ⓑ All positive integers only
Ⓒ All positive and negative integers, but not 0
Ⓓ All real numbers

8. **Which of the following is the same as 4 + (x − 3)?**

Ⓐ 4 + (−x) − 3
Ⓑ (−4) + x + (−3)
Ⓒ 4 + x + (−3)
Ⓓ 1 + (−x)

9. **Which of the following expressions represents the distance between the two points?**

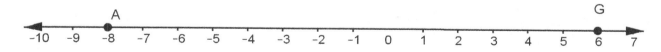

Ⓐ |6-8|
Ⓑ (- 8)+6
Ⓒ (- 8)- 6
Ⓓ |6 - (- 8)|

10. **Which words best complete the statement?**

The distance between two numbers on a number line is the same as the _____ of their _____.

Ⓐ Absolute value; difference
Ⓑ Sum; squares
Ⓒ Difference; squares
Ⓓ Absolute value; sum

11. **Use the number line to determine the distance between** $-1\dfrac{1}{6}$ **and** $\dfrac{5}{6}$ **. Write your answer in simplest form in the box given below.**

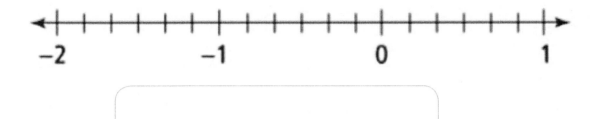

12. **Which of these situations can be represented by the opposite of 34?**

Instruction: More than one option may be correct.

Ⓐ The airplane ascends 34 feet.
Ⓑ The elevator descends 34 feet.
Ⓒ The cost of the coat is $34 more than expected.
Ⓓ Jack removes 34 books from the library shelf.

13. **State whether a number and its inverse are added in these expressions. If yes, select additive inverse is added. If no, select additive inverse is not added.**

	Additive Inverse is added	Additive Inverse is not added
$3 + (-3)$	○	○
$-2.2 + 2.2$	○	○
$1 + 1$	○	○
$-\dfrac{4}{7} + \left(-\dfrac{4}{7}\right)$	○	○

Chapter 3

Lesson 4: Strategies for Adding and Subtracting Rational Numbers

You can scan the QR code given below or use the url to access additional EdSearch resources including videos and mobile apps related to *Strategies for Adding and Subtracting Rational Numbers.*

 **Strategies for Adding and Subtracting Rational Numbers**

URL	QR Code
http://www.lumoslearning.com/a/7nsa1d	

1. **What property is illustrated in the equation?:**

$$7 + \frac{1}{2} = \frac{1}{2} + 7$$

   Ⓐ Commutative property of addition
   Ⓑ Associate property of addition
   Ⓒ Distributive property
   Ⓓ Identity property of addition

2. **Which is a valid use of properties to make the expression easier to calculate?**

   92 – 8 = ?

   Ⓐ 90 – 2 – 8
   Ⓑ 82 – (10 – 8)
   Ⓒ 82 + (10 – 8)
   Ⓓ (80 + 2) – 8

3. **Find the sum of the mixed numbers.**

$$4\frac{7}{8} + 7\frac{5}{8}$$

   Ⓐ $11\frac{5}{8}$

   Ⓑ $12\frac{1}{2}$

   Ⓒ $12\frac{7}{8}$

   Ⓓ $11\frac{1}{2}$

4. **Which is a correct use of the distributive property?**

   Ⓐ 3(4+2) = 3(4)+2
   Ⓑ 3(4+2) = (3 x 4) x (3 x 2)
   Ⓒ 3(4+2) = 3(4)+3(2)
   Ⓓ All of the above

5. Name the property illustrated in the equation:

(5 + 8) + 2 = 5 + (8 + 2)

- Ⓐ Distributive property
- Ⓑ Associative property of addition
- Ⓒ Commutative property of addition
- Ⓓ Identity property of addition

6. Which is a valid use of properties to make the expression easier to calculate?

7 – 2.45

- Ⓐ (6 – 2) + (1 – 0.45)
- Ⓑ (7 – 2) + 0.45
- Ⓒ 5 + 0.45
- Ⓓ 7 – (0.45 – 2)

7. Write the improper fraction as a mixed number.

$$\frac{31}{3}$$

- Ⓐ $3\frac{1}{3}$
- Ⓑ $30\frac{1}{3}$
- Ⓒ $31\frac{1}{3}$
- Ⓓ $10\frac{1}{3}$

8. Find the difference between $16\frac{3}{4}$ - $9\frac{7}{8}$

- Ⓐ $7\frac{1}{8}$
- Ⓑ $6\frac{7}{8}$
- Ⓒ $7\frac{7}{8}$
- Ⓓ $6\frac{1}{8}$

9. **What property is illustrated in the equation?:**

    (5 + 3) + 0 = 5 + 3

    Ⓐ Identity property of addition
    Ⓑ Associative property of addition
    Ⓒ Commutative property of addition
    Ⓓ Distributive property

10. **Which is a valid use of properties to make the expression easier to calculate? Circle the correct answer choice.**

    $$\frac{20}{7} - 1\frac{3}{7} =$$

    Ⓐ $\frac{20}{7} - 1 + \frac{3}{7}$

    Ⓑ $\frac{13}{7} - 1 + \frac{3}{7}$

    Ⓒ $\left(\frac{13}{7} - \frac{3}{7}\right) + (1 - 1)$

    Ⓓ $\frac{20}{7} - \frac{1}{7} - \frac{3}{7}$

11. **Which of the pairs of numbers are 13.7 units apart on a number line? More than 1 answer may be correct. Mark all the correct answers.**

    Ⓐ - 26.3 and - 12.6
    Ⓑ - 26.3 and 12.6
    Ⓒ 26.3 and - 12.6
    Ⓓ - 3.2 and 10.5

12. **Write the correct absolute value expression or distance description into the blanks in the table.**

Distance between 4 and -1	|-1-4|	|4-(-1)|
Distance between -4 and -1		|-4-(-1)|
Distance between 4 and 1	|1-4|	
	|1-(-4)|	|-4-1|

Chapter 3

Lesson 5: Rational Numbers, Multiplication and Division

You can scan the QR code given below or use the url to access additional EdSearch resources including videos and mobile apps related to *Rational Numbers, Multiplication and Division*.

 **Rational Numbers, Multiplication and Division**

URL	QR Code
http://www.lumoslearning.com/a/7nsa2	

1. **Fill in the blank to make a true equation.**

   (-9)*(___) = 36

   Ⓐ - 4
   Ⓑ 4
   Ⓒ 6
   Ⓓ - 6

2. **Solve for x.**

   x = (-2)(6)(-4)

   Ⓐ x = 36
   Ⓑ x = 0
   Ⓒ x = 48
   Ⓓ x = - 48

3. **Simplify the following complex fraction.**

   $$\dfrac{\dfrac{1}{2}}{\dfrac{2}{3}}$$

   Ⓐ $\dfrac{4}{3}$

   Ⓑ $\dfrac{1}{2}$

   Ⓒ $\dfrac{3}{4}$

   Ⓓ $\dfrac{4}{3}$

4. **Which of the following represents the product of 0.53 * 11.6?**

   Ⓐ 0.6148
   Ⓑ 6.148
   Ⓒ 61.48
   Ⓓ 614.8

5. **Which of the following is NOT a rational number?**

   Ⓐ $\dfrac{8}{15}$

   Ⓑ 20.6
   Ⓒ $\sqrt{3}$

   Ⓓ $\dfrac{9}{11}$

6. **Which of the following numbers is divisible by 3?**

   Ⓐ 459,732
   Ⓑ 129,682
   Ⓒ 1,999,000
   Ⓓ 5,684,722

7. **Which of the following fractions is equivalent to 0.625?**

   Ⓐ $\dfrac{7}{9}$

   Ⓑ $\dfrac{5}{8}$

   Ⓒ $\dfrac{2}{3}$

   Ⓓ $\dfrac{8}{9}$

8. Mary wanted to estimate how many sheets of paper she had left. She knew that each sheet was about 0.1 mm thick. Her pack measured 2 cm thick.

    Which is the best estimate of the number of sheets of paper in Mary's pack?

    Ⓐ 50
    Ⓑ 100
    Ⓒ 150
    Ⓓ 200

9. Which of the following is the multiplicative inverse of $\dfrac{-7}{9}$?

    Ⓐ $\dfrac{7}{9}$

    Ⓑ $\dfrac{-9}{7}$

    Ⓒ $\dfrac{9}{7}$

    Ⓓ 1

10. Determine how many steps are necessary in a stairway between two floors that are 10.5 feet apart if each step is 9 inches high.

    Ⓐ 11 steps
    Ⓑ 12 steps
    Ⓒ 13 steps
    Ⓓ 14 steps

11. Shade the figure given to represent $\dfrac{2}{10} + \dfrac{3}{10}$

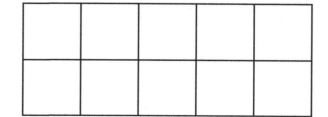

12. **Fill in the table with correct multiplication expression for each division expression or the correct division expression for each multiplication expression.**

Division Expression	Multiplication Expression
$\dfrac{\frac{-1}{3}}{\frac{7}{8}}$	$\dfrac{-1}{3} \times \dfrac{8}{7}$
$\dfrac{\frac{4}{3}}{-5}$	
$\dfrac{-6}{\frac{8}{9}}$	$-6 \times \dfrac{9}{8}$
	$\dfrac{-7}{3} \times \dfrac{9}{4}$
$\dfrac{\frac{-6}{11}}{\frac{-4}{5}}$	

13. **Which of the following products are positive? Select all the correct answer choices.**

Ⓐ $-\dfrac{2}{3} \times \dfrac{3}{4}$

Ⓑ $\dfrac{4}{5} \times \left(-\dfrac{2}{5}\right) \times (-3)$

Ⓒ $\left(-\dfrac{1}{8}\right)\left(-\dfrac{7}{8}\right)(10)$

Ⓓ $3\dfrac{4}{7} \times -2\dfrac{1}{2}$

Chapter 3

Lesson 6: Rational Numbers as Quotients of Integers

You can scan the QR code given below or use the url to access additional EdSearch resources including videos and mobile apps related to *Rational Numbers as Quotients of Integers*.

 **Rational Numbers as Quotients of Integers**

URL	QR Code
http://www.lumoslearning.com/a/7nsa2b	

1. **Which of the following division problems CANNOT be completed?**

    Ⓐ $10 \div 0$
    Ⓑ $155 \div (-3)$
    Ⓒ $\dfrac{2}{3} + \dfrac{1}{4}$
    Ⓓ $0 \div 5$

2. **Which of the following is NOT equivalent to the given value?:**

    $-\dfrac{2}{3}$

    Ⓐ $\dfrac{-2}{(3)}$

    Ⓑ $\dfrac{-2}{(-3)}$

    Ⓒ $\dfrac{2}{(-3)}$

    Ⓓ All are equivalent values

3. **Jared hiked a trail that is 12 miles long. He hiked the trail in section that were 1.5 miles each. In how many sections did he complete the hike?**

    Ⓐ 12
    Ⓑ 10
    Ⓒ 8
    Ⓓ 6

4. **Greg is able to run a mile in 8 minutes. He ran at that pace for t minutes. What does the following expression represent?**

    $\dfrac{t}{8}$

    Ⓐ The number of miles that Greg ran.
    Ⓑ The number of hours that Greg ran.
    Ⓒ The average pace at which Greg ran.
    Ⓓ The amount of time it took Greg to run 8 miles.

5. What value could x NOT be in the following expression?:

    $$\frac{5+x}{x}$$

    Ⓐ 5
    Ⓑ 1
    Ⓒ −5
    Ⓓ 0

6. Rose is filling her swimming pool with water. She needs to pump 2000 gallons into the pool, and the water flows at a rate of r gallons per hour. Which of the following expresses the amount of time it will take to fill the pool?

    Ⓐ $\dfrac{2000}{r}$

    Ⓑ 2000*r*

    Ⓒ 2000 + *r*

    Ⓓ $\dfrac{r}{2000}$

7. If t = −2, and v = −4, which of the following is equal to $\dfrac{t}{v}$?

    Ⓐ $\dfrac{t}{4}$

    Ⓑ $\dfrac{4}{2v}$

    Ⓒ $\dfrac{-t}{4}$

    Ⓓ $\dfrac{-6}{-3v}$

8. If , $\dfrac{3a}{b} = 12$, what is the value of $\left(-\dfrac{a}{b}\right)$?

Ⓐ - 4

Ⓑ $\dfrac{3}{4}$

Ⓒ $-\dfrac{3}{4}$

Ⓓ $\dfrac{1}{4}$

9. Which terms best complete the statement?

   A number is rational if it can be expressed as a _____ of _____.

   Ⓐ sum; integers
   Ⓑ quotient; integers
   Ⓒ difference; prime numbers
   Ⓓ product; variables

10. Kathy is laying stepping stones in her garden. The stones are 8 inches long, and she wants to create a path that is 10 feet long. How many stones will she need?

   Ⓐ 10 stones
   Ⓑ 80 stones
   Ⓒ 15 stones
   Ⓓ 1.25 stones

11. Complete the fraction: $\dfrac{?}{3} = -5$. Write your answer in the box given below.

12. Which of the quotients are equivalent to $-\dfrac{6}{7}$?

Note that more than one option may be correct. Select all the correct options.

Ⓐ $\dfrac{6}{7}$

Ⓑ $-\dfrac{-6}{7}$

Ⓒ $-\dfrac{-6}{-7}$

Ⓓ $\dfrac{-6}{-7}$

Ⓔ $\dfrac{6}{-7}$

Ⓕ $-\dfrac{6}{7}$

13. Mark the boxes to indicate whether the quotient is positive, negative, zero, or undefined.

	Positive	Negative	Zero	Undefined
$-50 \div 5$	○	○	○	○
$\dfrac{0}{-4}$	○	○	○	○
$\dfrac{-35}{-7}$	○	○	○	○
$\dfrac{47}{0}$	○	○	○	○

Chapter 3

Lesson 7: Strategies for Multiplying and Dividing Rational Numbers

You can scan the QR code given below or use the url to access additional EdSearch resources including videos and mobile apps related to *Strategies for Multiplying and Dividing Rational Numbers.*

 **Strategies for Multiplying and Dividing Rational Numbers**

URL	QR Code
http://www.lumoslearning.com/a/7nsa2c	

Name _____   Date _____

1. **Which of these multiplication expressions is equivalent to the division expression:**

$-\dfrac{4}{23} \div \dfrac{7}{58}$ **Circle the correct answer choice.**

Ⓐ $-\dfrac{23}{4} \times \dfrac{58}{7}$

Ⓑ $-\dfrac{4}{23} \times \dfrac{58}{7}$

Ⓒ $-\dfrac{23}{4} \times \dfrac{7}{58}$

Ⓓ $-\dfrac{4}{23} \times \dfrac{7}{58}$

2. **Which property is illustrated in the following statement?**

$(5)(4)(7) = (7)(5)(4)$

Ⓐ Triple multiplication property
Ⓑ Distributive property
Ⓒ Commutative property of multiplication
Ⓓ Associative property of multiplication

3. **Find the quotient:** $4 \div \dfrac{1}{2}$

Ⓐ 4
Ⓑ 8
Ⓒ 2
Ⓓ 16

4. **Which of the following is a helpful and valid way to rewrite the expression for evaluation :**

3(123)

Ⓐ 3(100) + 3(20) + 3(3)
Ⓑ 3(100) + 23
Ⓒ 100 + 3(23)
Ⓓ 300 + 3(20) + 3

5. Which multiplication expression are equivalent to $\dfrac{7}{8} \div \dfrac{1}{15}$?

Ⓐ $\dfrac{7}{8} \times 15$

Ⓑ $\dfrac{7}{8} \times \dfrac{1}{15}$

Ⓒ $\dfrac{8}{7} \div \dfrac{1}{15}$

Ⓓ $\dfrac{8}{7} \times \dfrac{1}{15}$

6. Which property is illustrated in the following statement?

$(2 \cdot 3) \cdot 6 = 2 \cdot (3 \cdot 6)$

Ⓐ Associate property of multiplication
Ⓑ Commutative property of multiplication
Ⓒ Identity property of multiplication
Ⓓ Reflexive property

7. Find the product: $\dfrac{3}{2} \star \dfrac{7}{6}$

Ⓐ $\dfrac{10}{12}$

Ⓑ $\dfrac{21}{6}$

Ⓒ $\dfrac{7}{4}$

Ⓓ $\dfrac{10}{8}$

Name _____

Date _____

8. **Find the quotient:** $\dfrac{6}{5} \div \dfrac{3}{25}$

Ⓐ $\dfrac{2}{5}$

Ⓑ 2

Ⓒ $\dfrac{5}{2}$

Ⓓ 10

9. **Find the product:** $\left(2\,\dfrac{1}{3} \right)\left(3\,\dfrac{1}{2} \right)$

Ⓐ $\dfrac{49}{6}$

Ⓑ $6\,\dfrac{1}{6}$

Ⓒ $\dfrac{6}{5}$

Ⓓ $5\,\dfrac{2}{5}$

10. **Find the quotient:** $\left(5\,\dfrac{1}{4} \right) \div \left(1\,\dfrac{1}{2} \right)$

Ⓐ $\dfrac{5}{8}$

Ⓑ $\dfrac{7}{2}$

Ⓒ 45

Ⓓ 7

11. Fill in the table with the correct reciprocals.

$\dfrac{6}{4}$	$\dfrac{4}{6}$
	$\dfrac{-19}{6}$
$\dfrac{5}{-64}$	
	4

Chapter 3

Lesson 8: Converting Between Rational Numbers and Decimals

You can scan the QR code given below or use the url to access additional EdSearch resources including videos and mobile apps related to *Converting Between Rational Numbers and Decimals*.

 **Search** **Converting Between Rational Numbers and Decimals**

URL	QR Code
http://www.lumoslearning.com/a/7nsa2d	

1. **Convert to a decimal:** $\dfrac{7}{8}$

   Ⓐ 0.78
   Ⓑ 0.81
   Ⓒ 0.875
   Ⓓ 0.925

2. **Convert to a decimal:** $\dfrac{5}{6}$

   Ⓐ 0.8333333...
   Ⓑ 0.56
   Ⓒ 0.94
   Ⓓ 0.8

3. **How can you tell that the following number is a rational number?**

   0.251

   Ⓐ It is a rational number because the decimal terminates.
   Ⓑ It is a rational number because there is a value of 0 in the ones place.
   Ⓒ It is a rational number because the sum of the digits is less than 10.
   Ⓓ It is a rational number because it is not a repeating decimal.

4. **A group of 11 friends ordered 4 pizzas to share. They divided the pizzas up evenly and all ate the same amount. Express in decimal form the portion of a pizza that each friend ate.**

   Ⓐ 0.36363636...
   Ⓑ 0.411
   Ⓒ 0.14141414...
   Ⓓ 0.48

5. **How can you tell that the following number is a rational number?**

   0.133333...

   Ⓐ It is rational because the decimal does not terminate.
   Ⓑ It is rational because the decimal repeats over and over.
   Ⓒ It is rational because the number is a factor of 1.
   Ⓓ It is NOT rational because the decimal does not terminate.

6. Convert to a decimal: $2\dfrac{2}{9}$

Ⓐ 2.92299229...
Ⓑ 2.2222...
Ⓒ 2.35
Ⓓ 2.4835

7. How can you tell that the following number is not a rational number?:

2.4876352586582142597868...

Ⓐ It is not rational because the same digit never occurs twice in a row in the decimal.
Ⓑ It is not rational because the decimal does not terminate or repeat.
Ⓒ It is not rational because it is greater than 1.
Ⓓ It is not rational because it is not a factor of 5.

8. Convert to a decimal: $\dfrac{11}{25}$

Ⓐ 0.4444444...
Ⓑ 0.472
Ⓒ 0.369
Ⓓ 0.44

9. The track at Haley's school is a third of a mile in length. She ran 14 laps on it after school one day. Express the number of miles she ran in decimal form.

Ⓐ 4.56
Ⓑ 3.85
Ⓒ 4.6666...
Ⓓ 4.725

10. Convert to a decimal: $\dfrac{34}{99}$

Ⓐ 0.943
Ⓑ 0.343434...
Ⓒ 0.394
Ⓓ 0.439439...

11. In the library, there are 230 fiction books, 120 nonfiction books, and 30 magazines. Write the ratio of magazines to nonfiction books as a decimal in the box given below.

12. **Which of the below statements are true? Select all the correct answer choices.**

Ⓐ $\frac{1}{4}$, 0.25, and 25% are equivalent

Ⓑ $\frac{1}{5}$, 0.20, and 20% are equivalent

Ⓒ $\frac{1}{4}$, 0.14, and 14% are equivalent

Ⓓ $\frac{1}{5}$, 0.20, and 2% are equivalent

Ⓔ $\frac{1}{4}$, 0.25, and 2.5% are equivalent

13. **Convert the rational numbers to decimals. Mark whether the decimals are repeating decimals or terminating decimals.**

	Repeating Decimal	Terminating Decimal
$\frac{3}{4}$	◯	◯
$\frac{2}{3}$	◯	◯
$\frac{1}{9}$	◯	◯
$\frac{2}{8}$	◯	◯

Chapter 3

Lesson 9: Solving Real World Problems

You can scan the QR code given below or use the url to access additional EdSearch resources including videos and mobile apps related to *Solving Real World Problems*.

 Solving Real World Problems

URL	QR Code
http://www.lumoslearning.com/a/7nsa3	

1. **Andrew has $9.39 but needs $15.00 to make a purchase. How much more does he need?**

    Ⓐ $6.39
    Ⓑ $5.61
    Ⓒ $5.39
    Ⓓ $6.61

2. **Ben has to unload a truck filled with 25 bags of grain for his horses. Each bag weighs 50.75 pounds.**

    How many total pounds does he have to move?

    Ⓐ 12,687.50 pounds
    Ⓑ 1,268.75 pounds
    Ⓒ 126.875 pounds
    Ⓓ 1250 pounds

3. **A Chinese restaurant purchased 1528.80 pounds of rice. If they received 50 identical bags, how much rice was in each bag?**

    Ⓐ 30.576 pounds
    Ⓑ 305.76 pounds
    Ⓒ 3.0576 pounds
    Ⓓ None of the above.

4. **Leila stopped at the coffee shop on her way to work. She ordered 2 bagels, 3 yogurts, and 1 orange juice. Bagels were $0.69 each, yogurts were $1.49 each, and orange juice was $1.75. What was Leila's total bill?**

    Ⓐ $7.60
    Ⓑ $3.93
    Ⓒ $5.16
    Ⓓ $5.42

5. **Mickey bought pizza and sodas for himself and four of his friends. The pizza was $17.49, and 5 sodas were $1.19 each.**

    If the pizza is sliced into 10 equal slices and each person eats 2 slices and drinks one soda, what is the cost to each person?

    Ⓐ $2.94
    Ⓑ $4.13
    Ⓒ $3.50
    Ⓓ $4.69

6. Alan has to keep within a $15.00 budget. Tax is 6.5%. What is Alan's total if he buys 1 notebook, 1 pack of paper, 1 set of dividers, 2 pens and 5 pencils?

3-Ring Notebook	$5.69
Notebook Paper	$1.39
Dividers	$1.45
Pens	$1.19
Pencils	$0.50

Ⓐ $10.88
Ⓑ $14.28
Ⓒ $13.41
Ⓓ $15.00

7. Sammy is mowing the lawn. The lawn is 30 ft by 20 ft. Sammy cut a strip 5 ft by 10 ft and ran out of gas. How much more does he need to mow?

Ⓐ 250 sq ft
Ⓑ 550 sq ft
Ⓒ 50 sq ft
Ⓓ 600 sq ft

8. Dustin has leased 5 acres of land to raise produce for the farmers' market. He has already planted $\frac{5}{8}$ of the land.

How many more acres does he need to plant?

Ⓐ $3\frac{1}{8}$ acres
Ⓑ 4 acres
Ⓒ $1\frac{7}{8}$ acres
Ⓓ $\frac{3}{8}$ acres

9. Taylor bought a bag of marbles weighing 5.25 lb. Before he got to the car, the bag broke, spilling many marbles. To find out if he had recovered all of his marbles, he weighed the bag at home.

He found that his bag of marbles now weighed 4.98 lb. What was the weight of the lost marbles?

Ⓐ 0.27 lb
Ⓑ 2.7 lb
Ⓒ 0.173 lb
Ⓓ 1.73 lb

10. Which of the following is a correct statement about the multiplication of two integers?

Ⓐ If the signs are both negative, multiply the numbers and give the answer a negative sign.
Ⓑ If the signs are both negative, multiply the numbers and give the answer a positive sign.
Ⓒ If the signs are unlike, multiply the numbers and give the answer a positive sign.
Ⓓ If the signs are unlike, multiply the numbers and give the answer the sign of the larger absolute value.

11. Robert has $\frac{4}{7}$ of a bucket of water. John has $\frac{2}{3}$ of a bucket of water. If Robert and John combine their buckets of water, how many buckets of water will they have? Write your answer in simplest form. Write your answer in the box given below.

12. Frank lives $\frac{1}{2}$ blocks east of Mary. Mary lives $\frac{3}{5}$ blocks east of school. How many blocks east of school does Frank live? There can be more than 1 correct answer. Select all the correct ones.

Ⓐ $1\frac{1}{10}$

Ⓑ $\frac{11}{10}$

Ⓒ $\frac{3}{5}$

Ⓓ $\frac{4}{2}$

Ⓔ $\frac{4}{7}$

13. Solve each equation and mark if the answer is negative, positive or zero.

	Negative	Zero	Positive
$-\frac{6}{7} - \left(-\frac{6}{7}\right)$	&#9711;	&#9711;	&#9711;
$-5 - \frac{3}{5}$	&#9711;	&#9711;	&#9711;
$\frac{3}{4} - \frac{1}{5}$	&#9711;	&#9711;	&#9711;

End of The Number System

Chapter 4:
Expressions and Equations

Lesson 1: Applying Properties to Rational Expressions

You can scan the QR code given below or use the url to access additional EdSearch resources including videos and mobile apps related to *Applying Properties to Rational Expressions*.

1. Ruby is two years younger than her brother. If Ruby's brother's age is A, which of the following expressions correctly represents Ruby's age?

    (A) A - 2
    (B) A + 2
    (C) 2A
    (D) 2 - A

2. Find the difference: 8n - (3n - 6) =

    (A) -n
    (B) 5n - 6
    (C) 5n + 6
    (D) 8n - 6

3. Find the sum:

    6t + (3t - 5) =

    (A) 9t - 5
    (B) 9t + 5
    (C) 3t - 5
    (D) 6t - 5

4. Combine like terms and factor the following expression.

    7x - 14x + 21x - 2

    (A) 15x - 2
    (B) 2(7x - 1)
    (C) 42x - 2
    (D) 21(x - 1)

5. Which of the following expressions is equivalent to:

    3(x + 4) - 2

    (A) 3x + 10
    (B) 3x + 14
    (C) 3x + 4
    (D) 3x + 5

6. **Simplify the following expression:**

$$\left(\frac{1}{2}\right)x + \left(\frac{3}{2}\right)x$$

Ⓐ 2x

Ⓑ $\left(\dfrac{5}{2}\right)$ x

Ⓒ - x

Ⓓ $\dfrac{x}{2}$

7. **Simplify the following expression:**

0.25x + 3 - 0.5x + 2

Ⓐ -0.25x + 5
Ⓑ 0.75x + 5
Ⓒ -0.25x + 1
Ⓓ 5.75x

8. **Which of the following statements correctly describes this expression?**

2x + 4

Ⓐ Four times a number plus two
Ⓑ Two more than four times a number
Ⓒ Four more than twice a number
Ⓓ Twice a number less four

9. Which of the following statements correctly describes the following expression?

$$\frac{2x - 3}{2}$$

  Ⓐ Half of three less than twice a number
  Ⓑ Half of twice a number
  Ⓒ Half of three less than a number
  Ⓓ Three less than twice a number

10. Which of the following expressions is not equivalent to:

$$(\frac{1}{2})(2x + 4) - 3$$

  Ⓐ $(x + 2) - 3$

  Ⓑ $(\frac{1}{2})(2x + 4) - 3$

  Ⓒ $x - 1$
  Ⓓ $x + 1$

11. Which property is demonstrated in the following expression?

  $12(3x - 9) = 36x - 108$

  Ⓐ Associative property
  Ⓑ Distributive property
  Ⓒ Identity property of addition
  Ⓓ Zero property of multiplication

12. Rhonda is purchasing fencing to go around a rectangular lot which is 4x + 9 ft long and 3x - 5 ft wide. Which expression represents the amount of fencing she must buy?

  Ⓐ $7x + 4$
  Ⓑ $7x - 4$
  Ⓒ $14x + 28$
  Ⓓ $14x + 8$

13. Rebekah is preparing for a swim meet. She is trying to swim 1 mile in 7 minutes. If the pool is 5x + 3 ft long, which expression represents how many laps she needs to swim in 7 minutes?

Assume 1 length of the pool is 1 lap. (1mile = 5280 feet.)

Ⓐ 7(5x + 3)

Ⓑ 5x + 3

Ⓒ $\dfrac{5280}{5x + 3}$

Ⓓ 5280(5x + 3)

14. Simplify.

5x + 10y + 0(z) =

Ⓐ 0

Ⓑ 5x + 10y

Ⓒ 15xy

Ⓓ 5x

15. Which property is demonstrated below?

2 + (8 + 3) = (2 + 8) + 3

Ⓐ Additive Identity Property

Ⓑ Multiplicative Identity Property

Ⓒ Distributive Property

Ⓓ Associative Property of Addition

16. Use the Distributive Property to expand the expression 6(5x – 3). Write your answer in the box given below.

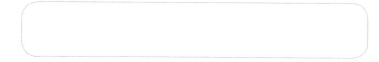

17. Which expressions are equal to 60x - 24? There is more than one correct answer. Select all the correct expressions.

Ⓐ 10(6x - 2)

Ⓑ 4(10x - 6)

Ⓒ 5(12x - 5)

Ⓓ 6(10x - 4)

Ⓔ -6(-10x + 4)

Ⓕ 4(15x - 6)

18. A bookstore is advertising $2 off the price of each book. You decide to buy 8 books. Let p represent the price of each book. Use the expression 8(p – 2) to find out how much you would spend if the regular price of each book is $13.

Write your answer in the box given below.

Chapter 4

Lesson 2: Interpreting the Meanings of Expressions

You can scan the QR code given below or use the url to access additional EdSearch resources including videos and mobile apps related to *Interpreting the Meanings of Expressions*.

 Search **Interpreting the Meanings of Expressions**

URL	QR Code
http://www.lumoslearning.com/a/7eea2	

1. **Which of the following expressions represents "5% of a number"?**

    Ⓐ 5n
    Ⓑ 0.5n
    Ⓒ 0.05n
    Ⓓ 500n

2. **Jill is shopping at a department store that is having a sale this week. The store has advertised 15% off certain off-season merchandise. Jill calculates the sales price by multiplying the regular price by 15% and then subtracting that amount from the regular price: SP = RP - 0.15(RP), where SP = Sales Price and RP = Regular Price. Find a simpler way for Jill to calculate the sales price as she shops.**

    Ⓐ SP = 0.15 RP
    Ⓑ SP = 1.15 RP
    Ⓒ SP = 0.85 RP
    Ⓓ SP = 1.85 RP

3. **Rewrite the following expression for the perimeter of a rectangle.**

    P = l + w + l + w, where P = perimeter, l = length, and w = width.

    Ⓐ P = l + 2w
    Ⓑ P = l + w
    Ⓒ P = 2(l) + w
    Ⓓ P = 2(l + w)

4. **If an item costs a store x dollars to buy and can be sold at y dollars, what percentage of the sale price is profit?**

    percentage of the sale price = [profit ÷ sale price] 100

    Which of the following rewrites this expression and includes the given information?

    Ⓐ $\dfrac{y - x}{100y}$

    Ⓑ $\dfrac{100(y - x)}{y}$

    Ⓒ $\dfrac{x - y}{100y}$

    Ⓓ $\dfrac{100(x - y)}{y}$

5. To find the average of five consecutive integers beginning with x, we add the integers and divide by 5.

Expressed in mathematical symbols, we have (x + x + 1+ x + 2 + x + 3 + x + 4) / 5 = Average (a)

Rewrite this expression another way.

Ⓐ x + 4
Ⓑ x + 3
Ⓒ x + 2
Ⓓ None of the above.

6   The bank will charge a 10% overdraft fee for any money withdrawn over the amount available in an account. If Jared has d dollars in the bank and he withdraws (d + 5) dollars, the bank charges 0.10{(d + 5) - d}. Find a simpler way of rewriting his overdraft fee.

Ⓐ 0.10(d + 5)
Ⓑ $0.50
Ⓒ $5.00
Ⓓ $2.50

7. Bob has been logging the days that the temperature rises over 100° in Orlando. He found that on 18 of the past 30 days the temperature rose above 100°.

Using this information, he made the following prediction of the number of days out of the next n days that the temperature would NOT rise above 100°:

$P = \left| \dfrac{30 - 18}{30} \right|$ n days. Find another way to write this expression.

Ⓐ $\left(\dfrac{2}{5}\right)$ n days

Ⓑ $\left(\dfrac{3}{5}\right)$ n days

Ⓒ $\left(\dfrac{4}{5}\right)$ n days

Ⓓ n days

8. If Roni runs for 20 minutes, walks for 10 and then runs for 15 while covering a total distance of m miles, her rate would be represented by:

r = m /{(20 + 10 +15) / 60} mph. Which of the following is a simpler representation of this formula?

Ⓐ r =(m/45) mph
Ⓑ r = (4/3m) mph
Ⓒ r = (45m/60) mph
Ⓓ r = (4m/3) mph

9. Hannah is taking piano lessons. Her mother has told her that each week she takes lessons, she has to practice $\frac{1}{2}$ hour more than she did the week before. Hannah created the following table. Write a simple expression to find the time she will practice in week 5n?

Piano Practice Time Sheet

Week	Time
1	1
2	1 1/2
n	1 + (1/2) (n-1)

Ⓐ $\frac{1 + 5n}{2}$ hr.

Ⓑ $\frac{5n}{2}$ hr.

Ⓒ $\frac{5n - 1}{2}$ hr.

Ⓓ $1 + \frac{5n}{2}$ hr.

10. The diameter of the Sun at the equator is 1,400,000 km. d = 1,400,000 km

Which of the following is another way to write this expression?

Ⓐ $d = 1.4 \times 10^6$ km
Ⓑ $d = 1.4 \times 10^{-6}$ km
Ⓒ $d = 14 \times 10^6$ km
Ⓓ $d = 14 \times 10^{-6}$ km

11. Which is another way of writing the following mathematical expression?

(6x - 15y - 2x + y) / -4(x - y)

Ⓐ $\frac{2x - 7y}{-2x - 2y}$

Ⓑ $\frac{2x - 7y}{-2}$

Ⓒ 5/2

Ⓓ $\frac{2x - 7y}{-2(x-y)}$

12. Which of the following expressions represents "a 24% increase"?

Ⓐ n + 0.24
Ⓑ n + 0.24n
Ⓒ n + 24
Ⓓ n + 24n

13. Ted is monitoring the scores of his two favorite football teams. He has a bet that Team A will finish with 19 points ahead of Team B.
He has made the following statement: Team A score -19 = Team B score. Which of the following is another way of making the same statement?

Ⓐ Team B Score - 19 points = Team A Score
Ⓑ Team B Score / Team A Score = 19 points
Ⓒ Team A Score + Team B Score = 19 points
Ⓓ Team A Score = Team B Score + 19 points

14. Linda bought 3 packages of red/white/blue ribbon for a rally. Each package held 3 rolls at 50 yd long and 3 rolls at 25 yd long, and each package cost $6.99.

Cost / yd = [3($6.99)] / 3[3(50) + 3(25)]

What is the cost/yd?

Ⓐ $0.031/yd
Ⓑ $0.31/yd
Ⓒ $3.10/yd
Ⓓ $2.10/yd

15. Jack went to the feed store to buy grain for his livestock. He bought fifty-five 50 lb bags.

Cost = $40/bag, but for every 10 bags, he got 1 free.

The following mathematical expression shows the cost/lb.

Cost/lb=$40(50)/[50(50) + 5(50)]

Which of the following is a simpler way of writing the above expression?

Ⓐ Cost/lb = $50(50) / [40(55)]
Ⓑ Cost/lb = $50(50) / [40(50)]
Ⓒ Cost/lb = $40(55) / [50(50)]
Ⓓ Cost/lb = $40(50) / [55(50)]

16. Sarah received a coupon for 15% off the total purchase price at a shoe store. Let p be the original price of the purchase. Use the expression p – 0.15p for the new price of the purchase. Write an equivalent expression by combining like terms.

17. Which of the expressions have like terms? There are more than 1 correct answer. Select all the correct answer choices

Ⓐ 4xy - 8y

Ⓑ -7x + 3x

Ⓒ h + 9.3h

Ⓓ 5t + 5

Ⓔ 12df - 3df

Ⓕ 8x - 2y

Chapter 4

Lesson 3: Modeling Using Equations or Inequalities

You can scan the QR code given below or use the url to access additional EdSearch resources including videos and mobile apps related to *Modeling Using Equations or Inequalities*.

 Search *Modeling Using Equations or Inequalities*

URL	QR Code
http://www.lumoslearning.com/a/7eeb4	

1. A 30 gallon overhead tank was slowly filled with water through a tap. The amount of water (W, in gallons) that is filled over a period of t hours can be found using W = 3.75(t). If the tap is opened at 7 AM and closed at 3 PM, how much water would be in the tank? Assume that the tank is empty before opening the tap.

    Ⓐ 18 gallons
    Ⓑ 20 gallons
    Ⓒ 24 gallons
    Ⓓ The tank is full

2. The ratio (by volume) of milk to water in a certain solution is 3 to 8. If the total volume of the solution is 187 cubic feet, what is the volume of water in the solution?

    Ⓐ 130 cubic feet
    Ⓑ 132 cubic feet
    Ⓒ 134 cubic feet
    Ⓓ 136 cubic feet

3. A box has a length of 12 inches and width of 10 inches. If the volume of the box is 960 cubic inches, what is its height?

    Ⓐ 6 inches
    Ⓑ 10 inches
    Ⓒ 12 inches
    Ⓓ 8 inches

4. Jan is planting tomato plants in her garden. Last year she planted 24 plants and harvested 12 bushels of tomatoes during the season. This year she has decided to only plant 18 plants. If the number of plants is directly proportional to the number of bushels of tomatoes harvested, how many bushels of tomatoes should she expect this year?

    Ⓐ 6
    Ⓑ 18
    Ⓒ 12
    Ⓓ 9

5. Melanie's age added to Roni's age is 27. Roni's age subtracted from Melanie's age is 3. Find their ages.

    Ⓐ 17, 10
    Ⓑ 16, 11
    Ⓒ 15, 12
    Ⓓ 14, 13

6. Tim wraps presents at a local gift shop. If it takes 2.5 meters of wrapping paper per present, how many can Tim wrap if he has 50 meters of wrapping paper?

   Ⓐ 18
   Ⓑ 20
   Ⓒ 15
   Ⓓ 17

7. Name the property demonstrated by the equation.

   11 + (8 + 6) = (y + 8) + 6. And find the value of y?

   Ⓐ 11, Commutative Property of Addition
   Ⓑ 11, Associative Property of Addition
   Ⓒ 11, Distributive Property
   Ⓓ 11, Associative Property of Multiplication

8. In the linear equation p = 2c + 1, c represents the number of couples attending a certain event, and p represents the number of people at that event.

   If there are 7 couples attending, how many people will be present?

   Ⓐ 7 people
   Ⓑ 14 people
   Ⓒ 15 people
   Ⓓ 16 people

9. The ratio (by volume) of salt to sugar in a certain mixture is 4 to 8. If the total volume of the mixture is 300 cubic feet, what is the volume of sugar in the mixture?

   Ⓐ 200 cubic feet
   Ⓑ 199 cubic feet
   Ⓒ 201 cubic feet
   Ⓓ 136 cubic feet

10. Which of the following sequences follows the rule $(8 + t^2) - 2t$ where t is equal to the number's position in the sequence?

    Ⓐ 7, 8, 11, 16, 23, ...
    Ⓑ 9, 12, 17, 24, 33 ...
    Ⓒ 3, 4, 5, 6, 7, ...
    Ⓓ 7, 10, 15, 22, 31, ...

11. Use the model to solve the equation. Circle the correct answer choice.

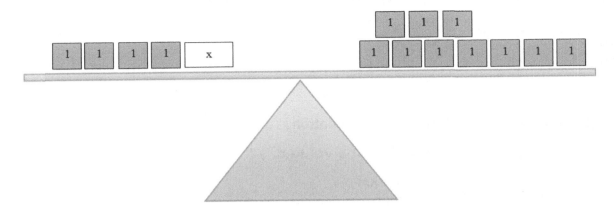

ⓐ 6
ⓑ 4
ⓒ 1
ⓓ 10

12. Which equation correctly represents the model and what is the solution?

Note: Select the answers that have the correct equation and solution. There is more than one correct answer.

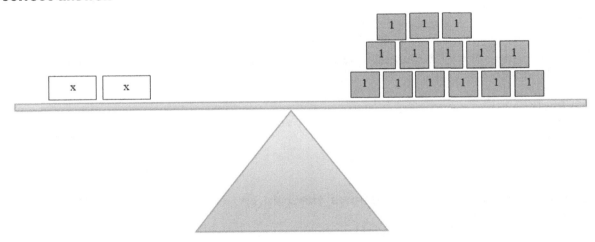

ⓐ 2x = 14 and x = 7
ⓑ x + 2 = 14 and x = 12
ⓒ 2 + x = 14 and x = 12
ⓓ x + x = 14 and x = 7
ⓔ 2 = 14x and x = 0.5

Chapter 4

Lesson 4: Solving Multi-Step Problems

You can scan the QR code given below or use the url to access additional EdSearch resources including videos and mobile apps related to *Interpreting the Meanings of Expressions*.

 Solving Multi-Step Problems

URL	QR Code
http://www.lumoslearning.com/a/7eeb3	

1. Bob, the plumber, charges $\frac{1}{4}$ the cost of materials as his labor fee. If his current job has a material cost of $130, how much will Bob charge his client (including his labor fee)?

   (A) $162.50
   (B) $32.50
   (C) $130.25
   (D) None of the above

2. A box has a length of 6x inches. The width equals one third the length, and the height equals half the length. If the volume equals 972 cubic inches, what does x equal?

   (A) 5
   (B) 2
   (C) 3
   (D) 4

3. Taylor is trimming the shrubbery along three sides of his backyard. The backyard is rectangular in shape. The length of the backyard is twice its width and the total perimeter is 180 feet.

   The shrubbery that Taylor needs to trim is along three sides of the rectangular backyard (along the two lengths and one width). Find the total length of the shrubbery that he needs to trim.

   (A) 180 ft
   (B) 120 ft
   (C) 90 ft
   (D) 150 ft

4. Jim is 4 years older than his brother Bob. In two years, Jim will be twice Bob's age. How old are they now?

   (A) Bob is 6 and Jim is 10.
   (B) Bob is 4 and Jim is 8.
   (C) Bob is 0 and Jim is 4.
   (D) Bob is 2 and Jim is 6.

5. In a certain classroom, the ratio of boys to girls is 2 to 1. If there are 39 students in the classroom, how many are boys?

Ⓐ 18
Ⓑ 22
Ⓒ 26
Ⓓ 30

6. John put three gallons of gasoline into his truck. The gasoline level was at 10% before he added the gasoline. If the truck has a 12 gallon tank, how much more gasoline can fit in the tank?

Ⓐ 7.8 gallons
Ⓑ 6.7 gallons
Ⓒ 8.9 gallons
Ⓓ 10.8 gallons

7. Melanie has $35.00 in her savings account and does cleaning in a neighbor's house for $15.00 per week. Sue has no money saved, but is mowing lawns at $20.00 each. If Sue mows 1 lawn per week, how long will it take her to catch up with Melanie?

Ⓐ 5 weeks
Ⓑ 6 weeks
Ⓒ 7 weeks
Ⓓ 8 weeks

8. Sissy is baking cookies for her class party. She plans to bake 128 cookies. Her recipe makes 6 dozen cookies. If her recipe calls for 3 1/2 c flour, how much flour will she need to make 128 cookies (round to the nearest half cup)?

Ⓐ $5\frac{1}{2}$ c
Ⓑ 4 c
Ⓒ $4\frac{1}{2}$ c
Ⓓ 6 c

9. Jenn went to the farmer's market with $40.00. She bought a 10 lb bag of potatoes for $6.00, a pie for $8.00, 4 qt fresh blueberries for $4.00 per qt, and 5 lb of apples at $1.49 per lb. What percent of the $40.00 did she still have when she left?

Ⓐ 93.625%
Ⓑ 6.375%
Ⓒ 25%
Ⓓ .0595%

10. Nelly spent $\frac{7}{8}$ of his savings on furniture and the rest on a lawnmower. If the lawnmower cost him $250, how much did he spend on furniture?

Ⓐ $2000
Ⓑ $1750
Ⓒ $1500
Ⓓ $1000

11. What is the perimeter of a figure where the width is x and the length is x + 4? Select the correct expressions.

Note: There is more than one correct answer.

Ⓐ x + 8
Ⓑ (x + 4) + x
Ⓒ x + x + (x +4) + (x + 4)
Ⓓ 4x + 8
Ⓔ zx + 4

12. Lisa is buying wallpaper for her room. The wallpaper costs $3.50 per foot. The wallpaper company also charges a $5 delivery fee per order. Let f represent the number of feet of wallpaper needed. Write an expression to represent how much Lisa will spend.

13. Which expression is the product of two factors and is equivalent to 3x - 27. Circle the correct answer choice.

Ⓐ 3 (x - 9)
Ⓑ -3 (3x -9)
Ⓒ 8x (8x - 15)
Ⓓ 3x (9x8)

Chapter 4

Lesson 5: Linear Inequality Word Problems

You can scan the QR code given below or use the url to access additional EdSearch resources including videos and mobile apps related to *Linear Inequality Word Problems*.

 Search   **Linear Inequality Word Problems**

URL	QR Code
http://www.lumoslearning.com/a/7eeb4b	

1. The annual salary for a certain position depends upon the years of experience of the applicant. The base salary is $50,000, and an additional $3,000 is added to that per year of experience, y, in the field. The company does not want to pay more than $70,000 for this position, though. Which of the following inequalities correctly expresses this scenario?

    Ⓐ 53,000y ≤ 70,000
    Ⓑ 3,000y ≤ 50,000
    Ⓒ 50,000 + 3,000y ≤ 70,000
    Ⓓ 3,000 + 50,000y ≤ 70,000

2. Huck has $225 in savings, and he is able to save an additional $45 per week from his work income. He wants to save enough money to have at least $500 in his savings. If w is the number of weeks, express this situation as an inequality.

    Ⓐ 265w ≥ 500
    Ⓑ 225 + 45w ≥ 500
    Ⓒ 225 ≤ 45w
    Ⓓ 225 + 45w ≤ 500

3. Lucy is charging her phone. It has a 20% charge right now and increases by an additional 2% charge every 3 minutes. She doesn't want to take it off the charger until it is at least 75% charged. If m is the number of minutes Lucy keeps her phone for charging, express this situation in an inequality.

    Ⓐ $20 + \dfrac{2}{3} m \le 75$

    Ⓑ $20m + \dfrac{2}{3} m \le 75$

    Ⓒ $75 + \dfrac{2}{3} m \ge 20$

    Ⓓ $20 + \dfrac{2}{3} m \ge 75$

4. Matt's final grade, G, in class depends on his last test score, t, according to the expression G = 74 + 0.20t. If he wants to have a final grade of at least 90.0, what is the minimum score he can make on the test?

    Ⓐ 80
    Ⓑ 74
    Ⓒ 92
    Ⓓ 86

5. Students can figure out their grade, G, on the test based upon how many questions they miss, n. The formula for their grade is G = 100 – 4n. If Tim wants to make at least an 83, what is the maximum number of questions he can miss?

Ⓐ 5 questions
Ⓑ 3 questions
Ⓒ 4 questions
Ⓓ 6 questions

6. The necessary thickness, T, of a steel panel in mm depends on the unsupported length, L, of the panel in feet according to the inequality T ≥ 3 + 0.2L. If the thickest panel available has a thickness of 12 mm, what is the maximum length it can span?

Ⓐ 75 ft
Ⓑ 45 ft
Ⓒ 60 ft
Ⓓ 54 ft

7. The pay that a salesperson receives each week is represented by the inequality P ≥ 300 + 25s, where s represents the number of units the salesperson sells. What is the significance of the number 300 in this inequality in this context?

Ⓐ The salesperson will never make more than $300 weekly.
Ⓑ The salesperson has never sold more than 300 units in a week.
Ⓒ The salesperson is guaranteed at least $300 even if he doesn't sell any units.
Ⓓ $300 is the price of a single unit.

8. The net calories gained or lost by a dieter depends on the hours exercised in a week according to the equation C = 750 – 200h. Based on his goals, Neil determines that the following inequality is necessary for him: h > 3.75. What is the significance of the value of this inequality?

Ⓐ Neil will lose at least 3.75 pounds per week if he meets this inequality.
Ⓑ Neil will lose weight each week if he meets this inequality.
Ⓒ Neil can eat only 375 calories on any given day.
Ⓓ If Neil meets this inequality, he will be able to eat as many calories as he likes.

9. **A school always allows twice as many girls as boys to enroll in swimming classes each year. They also follow a certain inequality for the number of boys, B, and girls, G, in their admissions: B + G ≤ 300. What significance does this inequality have for the number of boys that can be admitted each year?**

Ⓐ At least 200 boys must be admitted.
Ⓑ No more than 100 boys can be admitted.
Ⓒ The number of boys admitted must equal the number of girls.
Ⓓ No more than 150 boys can be admitted.

10. **Isaac has to do at least 4 hours of chores each week. For each hour of television he watches, that minimum number of hours increases by 0.25. This week, the inequality for his hours of chores is h ≥ 5.5. What does this indicate about his television watching?**

Circle the correct answer choice.

Ⓐ He watched 6 hours of television this week.
Ⓑ He watched 5.5 hours of television this week.
Ⓒ He watched 22 hours of television this week.
Ⓓ He watched no television this week.

11. **The initial cost to rent a bike is $5. Each hour the bike is rented costs $2. Liz is going to rent a bike and can spend at most $17. Write and solve an inequality to find how long she can rent the bike.**

12. Some friends put their money together to buy frozen treats from an ice cream truck. Two people got popsicles. Two people got ice cream cones. Each ice cream cone costs twice as much as popsicle. Two people ordered double scoops. Each double scoop cost three times as much as a popsicle. The total cost for their treats was less than $24.12. What are two possible prices for a popsicle? Write and solve the inequality.

Ⓐ $2.03
Ⓑ $2.02
Ⓒ $2.01
Ⓓ $2.00
Ⓔ $1.95

13. A garden center sells 21 trays of red flowers, 12 trays of yellow flowers, and 16 trays of pink flowers every day. The gardener wants to know how many days, d, it will take to sell more than 200 trays of flowers. Which inequality models the situation.

Circle the correct answer choice.

Ⓐ 21d + 12d + 16d <200
Ⓑ 21d + 12d + 16d >200
Ⓒ 200 ≤ 21d + 16d + 12d
Ⓓ 200 ≥ 21d + 16d + 12d

End of Expressions and Equations

Chapter 5: Geometry

Lesson 1: Scale Models

You can scan the QR code given below or use the url to access additional EdSearch resources including videos and mobile apps related to *Scale Models*.

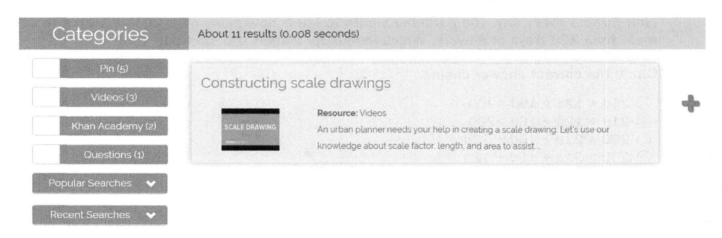

Categories

About 11 results (0.008 seconds)

- Pin (5)
- Videos (3)
- Khan Academy (2)
- Questions (1)
- Popular Searches ⌄
- Recent Searches ⌄

Constructing scale drawings

SCALE DRAWING

Resource: Videos

An urban planner needs your help in creating a scale drawing. Let's use our knowledge about scale factor, length, and area to assist...

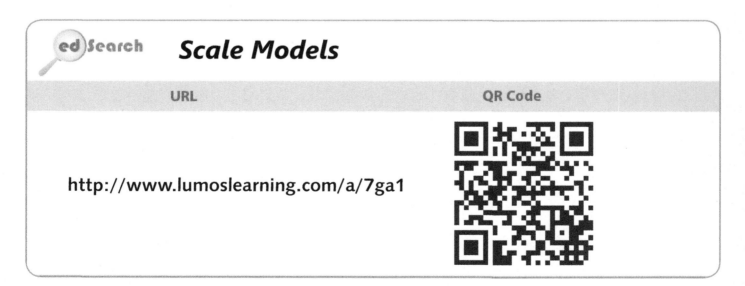

ed Search   *Scale Models*

URL	QR Code
http://www.lumoslearning.com/a/7ga1	

1. **Triangle ABC and triangle PQR are similar. Find the value of x.**

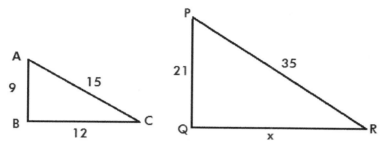

- Ⓐ 23
- Ⓑ 25
- Ⓒ 26
- Ⓓ 28

2. **If the sides of two similar figures have a similarity ratio of $\dfrac{3}{2}$ what is the ratio of their areas?**

- Ⓐ $\dfrac{9}{4}$

- Ⓑ $\dfrac{3}{2}$

- Ⓒ $\dfrac{1}{3}$

- Ⓓ $\dfrac{3}{1}$

3. **What is the similarity ratio between the following two similar figures?**

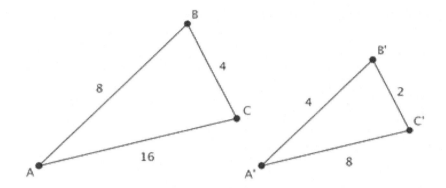

Ⓐ $\dfrac{2}{1}$

Ⓑ $\dfrac{1}{4}$

Ⓒ $\dfrac{2}{3}$

Ⓓ $\dfrac{3}{2}$

4. **A map is designed with a scale of 1 inch for every 5 miles. If the distance between two towns is 3 inches on the map, how far apart are they?**

Ⓐ 15 miles
Ⓑ 3 miles
Ⓒ 5 miles
Ⓓ 1.5 miles

5. **If the angles of one of two similar triangles are 30, 60, and 90 degrees, what are the angles for the other triangle?**

Ⓐ 60, 120, 180
Ⓑ 45, 45, 90
Ⓒ 30, 60, 90
Ⓓ There is not enough information to determine.

6. The ratio of similarity between two figures is $\dfrac{4}{3}$.

    If one side of the larger figure is 12 cm long, what is the length of the corresponding side in the smaller figure?

    Ⓐ 9 cm
    Ⓑ 16 cm
    Ⓒ 3 cm

    Ⓓ $\dfrac{4}{3}$ cm

7. If the sides of two similar figures have a similarity ratio of $\dfrac{5}{3}$ what is the ratio of their perimeters?

    Ⓐ $\dfrac{25}{9}$

    Ⓑ $\dfrac{5}{6}$

    Ⓒ $\dfrac{5}{3}$

    Ⓓ $\dfrac{3}{5}$

8. Triangle ABC and triangle DEF are similar. Find the value of x.

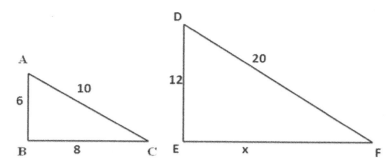

    Ⓐ 16
    Ⓑ 18
    Ⓒ 14
    Ⓓ 12

9. Triangle ABC and triangle DEF are similar. Find the value of x.

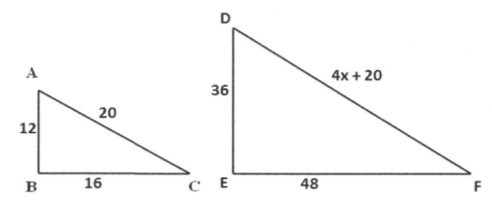

- Ⓐ 5
- Ⓑ 20
- Ⓒ 10
- Ⓓ 15

10. Triangle ABC and triangle DEF are similar. Find the value of x.

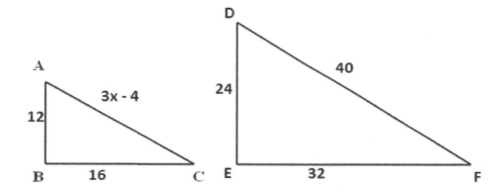

- Ⓐ 5
- Ⓑ 10
- Ⓒ 8
- Ⓓ 6

11. On a map, 1 inch equals 15 miles. Two cities are 6 inches apart on the map. What is the actual distance between the cities?

Write your answer in the box given below

12. On a map, 1.5 inches equals 150 miles. The distance that a man travels is 4 inches on the map. Represent the scale as two different ratios.

Note: Select two ratios that represent the scale of the map.

Ⓐ $\dfrac{150 \text{ miles}}{1.5 \text{ inches}}$

Ⓑ $\dfrac{1.5 \text{ inches}}{150 \text{ miles}}$

Ⓒ $\dfrac{4 \text{ inches}}{150 \text{ miles}}$

Ⓓ $\dfrac{150 \text{ miles}}{4 \text{ inches}}$

13. Mark the map with the correct scale for the situation described.

	Map 1 Scale is 1 in : 15 miles	Map 2 Scale is 2 in : 25 miles
Frank traveled an actual distance of 45 miles. On the map, he traveled 3 inches.	◯	◯
Two cities are 135 miles apart. On the map, they are 9 inches apart.	◯	◯
It is 137.5 miles from City 1 to City 2. On the map, City 1 and City 2 are 11 inches apart.	◯	◯
The map shows that the school and library are 5 inches apart. Therefore they are 62.5 miles apart.	◯	◯

Chapter 5

Lesson 2: Drawing Plane (2-D) Figures

You can scan the QR code given below or use the url to access additional EdSearch resources including videos and mobile apps related to *Drawing Plane (2-D) Figures*.

ed)Search *Drawing Plane (2-D) Figures*

URL	QR Code
http://www.lumoslearning.com/a/7ga2	

1. Which of the following lengths cannot be the lengths of the sides of a triangle?

   Ⓐ 4, 6, 9
   Ⓑ 3, 4, 2
   Ⓒ 2, 2, 3
   Ⓓ 1, 1, 2

2. Which of the following set of lengths cannot be the lengths of the sides of a triangle?

   Ⓐ 12.5, 20, 30
   Ⓑ 10, 10, 12
   Ⓒ 4, 8.5, 14
   Ⓓ 3, 3, 3

3. If the measure of two angles in a triangle are 60 and 100 degrees, what is the measure of the third angle?

   Ⓐ 20 degrees
   Ⓑ 50 degrees
   Ⓒ 30 degrees
   Ⓓ 180 degrees

4. Which of the following triangle classifications does not describe the angles in a triangle?

   Ⓐ Right
   Ⓑ Acute
   Ⓒ Equiangular
   Ⓓ Scalene

5. **Which of the angles has the least measure?**

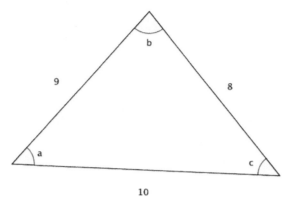

   Ⓐ a
   Ⓑ b
   Ⓒ c
   Ⓓ There is not enough information to tell

6. **Find the value of x.**

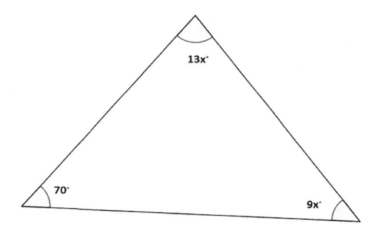

   Ⓐ 6
   Ⓑ 5
   Ⓒ 10
   Ⓓ 4

7. **Which of the following lengths cannot be the lengths of the sides of a triangle?**

   Ⓐ 8, 12, 18
   Ⓑ 6, 8, 4
   Ⓒ 4, 4, 6
   Ⓓ 2, 2, 4

8. If this is an isosceles triangle, which of the following could be the measure of each of the unknown angles? Take the sides which make up the angle 70° as equal to each other.

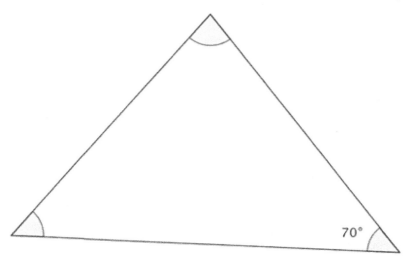

    Ⓐ 55°
    Ⓑ 66°
    Ⓒ 53°
    Ⓓ 70°

9. Which of the following triangle classification is defined by an angle that is created by two perpendicular lines?

    Ⓐ Right
    Ⓑ Acute
    Ⓒ Equiangular
    Ⓓ Scalene

10. Which of the following triangle classifications is defined by three angles less than 90 degrees?

    Ⓐ Right
    Ⓑ Acute
    Ⓒ Obtuse
    Ⓓ Scalene

11. Categorize the shapes as parallelograms and non-parallelograms.

	Non-Parallelogram	Parallelogram
Trapezoid	○	○
Rectangle	○	○
Square	○	○
Rhombus	○	○

12. Which of these quadrilaterals could have two sides with a length of 4 inches and and two sides with a length of 6 inches?

Select all the correct answers.

Ⓐ Parallelogram
Ⓑ Rhombus
Ⓒ Trapezoid
Ⓓ Rectangle

13. Which of these geometric shapes have exactly one pair of parallel sides?

Please write the correct answer from the list below into the box provided.

Rhombus

Triangle

Regular Octagon

Trapezoid

Chapter 5

Lesson 3: Cross Sections of 3-D Figures

You can scan the QR code given below or use the url to access additional EdSearch resources including videos and mobile apps related to *Cross Sections of 3-D Figures*.

 **Cross Sections of 3-D Figures**

URL	QR Code
http://www.lumoslearning.com/a/7ga3	

1. **The horizontal cross section of a square pyramid is a _____.**

   Ⓐ Square
   Ⓑ Circle
   Ⓒ Trapezoid
   Ⓓ Triangle

2. **In order for a three-dimensional shape to be classified as a "prism," its horizontal cross-sections must be _____.**

   Ⓐ congruent polygons
   Ⓑ non-congruent polygons
   Ⓒ circles
   Ⓓ equilateral triangles

3. **Which of the following nets is NOT the net of a cube?**

   Ⓐ

   Ⓑ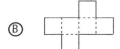

   Ⓒ

   Ⓓ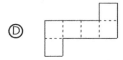

4. **The horizonal cross section of a pentagonal prism is a _____.**

   Ⓐ Triangle
   Ⓑ Pentagon
   Ⓒ Trapezoid
   Ⓓ Square

5. The vertical cross section of a cube is a _____.

   Ⓐ   Square
   Ⓑ   Triangle
   Ⓒ   Circle
   Ⓓ   Trapezoid

6. Which of the following shapes represents the sides of a pyramid?

   Ⓐ   Triangle
   Ⓑ   Rectangle
   Ⓒ   Trapezoid
   Ⓓ   Square

7. How many faces does a cube have?

   Ⓐ   4
   Ⓑ   2
   Ⓒ   6
   Ⓓ   8

8. Which of the following sets of information would not allow you to draw a unique triangle?

   Ⓐ   The length of the three sides
   Ⓑ   The length of two of the sides and the angle between them
   Ⓒ   The size of two angles and one of the sides
   Ⓓ   The length of two sides and an angle not between them

9. Which statement is not true?

   Ⓐ   The right cross section of a square pyramid is a trapezoid.
   Ⓑ   The vertical cross section of a square pyramid is a triangle.
   Ⓒ   The base of a square pyramid is a triangle.
   Ⓓ   The horizontal cross section of a square pyramid is a square.

10. Samuel and Christina made a model colonial-style house for their history class. The figures below show the top, side, and front views of the 2 three-dimensional figures they used to make their house.

Based on the figures, which two 3D figures did Samuel and Christina use?

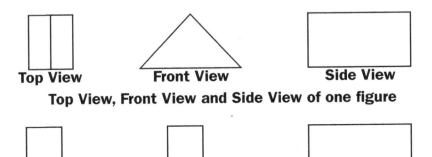

Top View   Front View   Side View

Top View, Front View and Side View of one figure

Top View   Front View   Side View

Top View, Front View and Side View of another figure

Ⓐ Triangular prism and cube
Ⓑ Rectangular prism and triangular prism
Ⓒ Triangular pyramid and triangular prism
Ⓓ Cube and triangular pyramid

11. What are the dimensions of a horizontal cross section of the rectangular prism? Remember that the figure is not drawn to scale.

Select all the correct answers.

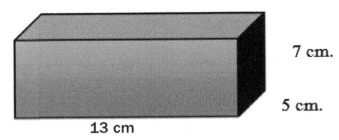

7 cm.

5 cm.

13 cm

Ⓐ 7 cm x 5 cm
Ⓑ 5 cm x 7 cm
Ⓒ 13 cm x 5 cm
Ⓓ 7 cm x 13 cm
Ⓔ 13 cm x 7 cm
Ⓕ 5 cm x 13 cm

12. What are the dimensions of a vertical cross section (Take the vertical plane cutting across the prism to be parallel to the right side face of the prism) of the rectangular prism? Remember that the figure is not drawn to scale.

Write your answer in the box given below.

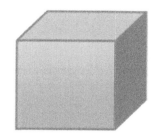

6 in.

3 in.

5 in.

13. Match the cross section with the description of the shape of the cross section.

	Rectangle	Square
Horizontal cross section of a rectangular prism	○	○
Vertical cross section of a rectangular prism	○	○
Horizontal cross section of a square pyramid	○	○
Vertical cross section of a cube	○	○

Chapter 5

Lesson 4: Circles

You can scan the QR code given below or use the url to access additional EdSearch resources including videos and mobile apps related to *Circles*.

 **Circles**

URL	QR Code
http://www.lumoslearning.com/a/7gb4	

1. A circle is divided into 4 equal sections. What is the measure of each of the angles formed at the center of the circle?

    Ⓐ 25°
    Ⓑ 180°
    Ⓒ 90°
    Ⓓ 360°

2. What is the area of a circle with diameter 8 cm? Round your answer to the nearest tenth. Use π = 3.14.

    Ⓐ 201.1 cm²
    Ⓑ 201.0 cm²
    Ⓒ 50.2 cm²
    Ⓓ 25.1 cm²

3. What is the radius of a circle with a circumference of 125 cm? Round your answer to the nearest whole number. Use π = 3.14.

    Ⓐ 24 cm
    Ⓑ 10 cm
    Ⓒ 20 cm
    Ⓓ 19 cm

4. What is the circumference of a circle with radius 0.5 feet? Round your answer to the nearest tenth. Use π = 3.14.

    Ⓐ 3.1 ft
    Ⓑ 3.2 ft
    Ⓒ 0.8 ft
    Ⓓ 0.7 ft

5. Which of the following could constitute the area of a circle?

    Ⓐ 50 units
    Ⓑ 1 square unit
    Ⓒ 1.5 cubic units
    Ⓓ One half of a unit

6. If two radii form a 30 degree angle at the center of a circle with radius 10 cm, what is the area between them? Round your answer to the nearest tenth. Use π = 3.14.

   Hint: A circle "sweeps out" 360 degrees.

   Ⓐ 26.2 square centimeters
   Ⓑ 26.1 square centimeters
   Ⓒ 314.1 square centimeters
   Ⓓ 314.2 square centimeters

7. What is the area of a circle with radius 2.8 cm? Round your answer to the nearest tenth. Use π = 3.14.

   Ⓐ 24.7 cm²
   Ⓑ 24.6 cm²
   Ⓒ 17.6 cm²
   Ⓓ 8.8 cm²

8. What is the radius of a circle with area 50 square cm? Round your answer to the nearest whole number. Use π = 3.14.

   Ⓐ 4 cm
   Ⓑ 3 cm
   Ⓒ 8 cm
   Ⓓ 7 cm

9. What is the length of a semi-circle (curved part only) with radius 8 in? Round your answer to the nearest tenth. Use π = 3.14.

   Hint: A semi-circle is half a circle.

   Ⓐ 201.0 in
   Ⓑ 50.2 in
   Ⓒ 100.5 in
   Ⓓ 25.1 in

10. What is the diameter of a circle with an area of 50.24 m²? Use π = 3.14.

   Ⓐ 4 m
   Ⓑ 6 m
   Ⓒ 8 m
   Ⓓ 16 m

11. A circular frisbee has a circumference of 15.2 inches. What is the area of this frisbee?

   Use 3.14 for pi. Round to the nearest whole number if needed.

12. Match the description with the correct radius that corresponds with the area or circumference. Use π = 3.14.

	Radius = 4in.	Radius = 5in.
The circumference of a circle is 31.4 in. Use 3.14 for π.	◯	◯
The area of a circle is 78.5 in². Use 3.14 for π.	◯	◯
The area of a circle is 50.24 in². Use 3.14 for π.	◯	◯
The circumference of a circle is 25.12 in. Use 3.14 for π.	◯	◯

13. What is the area of a circle with a diameter of 24in.?

   Use 3.14 for pi. Round to the nearest whole number if needed.

Chapter 5

Lesson 5: Angles

You can scan the QR code given below or use the url to access additional EdSearch resources including videos and mobile apps related to *Angles*.

 **Angles**

URL	QR Code
http://www.lumoslearning.com/a/7gb5	

1. **Find x.**

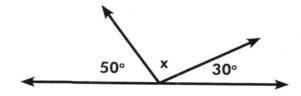

    Ⓐ   40°
    Ⓑ   60°
    Ⓒ   80°
    Ⓓ   100°

2. **Find the measures of the missing angles in the figure below.**

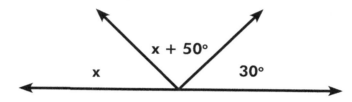

    Ⓐ   30° and 60°
    Ⓑ   60° and 90°
    Ⓒ   50° and 100°
    Ⓓ   60° and 120°

3. **The sum of the measures of angles a and b 155 degrees. What is the measure of angle b?**

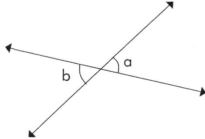

    Ⓐ   155 degrees
    Ⓑ   77.5 degrees
    Ⓒ   35 degrees
    Ⓓ   210.5 degrees

4. **What is true about every pair of vertical angles?**

   Ⓐ They are supplementary.
   Ⓑ They are complementary.
   Ⓒ They are equal in measure.
   Ⓓ They total 360 degrees.

5. **If the sum of the measures of two angles is 180 degrees, they are called —**

   Ⓐ supplementary angles
   Ⓑ complementary angles
   Ⓒ vertical angles
   Ⓓ equivalent angles

6. **If angle a measures 30 degrees, what is the measure of angle b?**

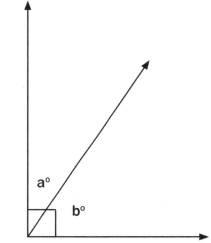

   Ⓐ 60 degrees
   Ⓑ 30 degrees
   Ⓒ 150 degrees
   Ⓓ 20 degrees

7. **If the measure of the first of two complementary angles is 68 degrees, what is the measure of the second angle?**

   Ⓐ 68 degrees
   Ⓑ 22 degrees
   Ⓒ 44 degrees
   Ⓓ 34 degrees

8. If the sum of the measures of angles a and b is 110 degrees, what is the measure of angle c?

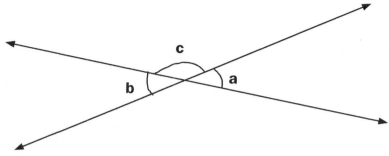

Ⓐ 125 degrees
Ⓑ 55 degrees
Ⓒ 70 degrees
Ⓓ 180 degrees

9. If two angles are both supplementary and equal in measure, they must be

Ⓐ vertical angles
Ⓑ right angles
Ⓒ adjacent angles
Ⓓ obtuse angles

10. If the sum of the measures of angles a and b is 240 degrees, what is the measure of angle c?

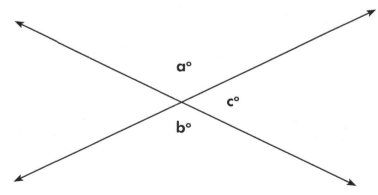

Ⓐ 60 degrees
Ⓑ 30 degrees
Ⓒ 160 degrees
Ⓓ 150 degrees

11. What is the measure of angle ∠A? Type the answer in the box.

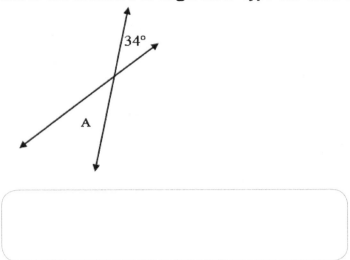

34°

A

12. What is the measure of angle ∠A? Type the answer in the box.

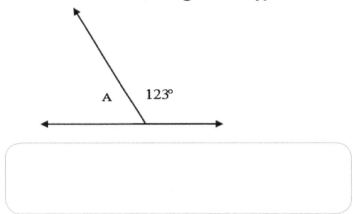

A   123°

13. What is the measure of angle ∠A? Type the answer in the box.

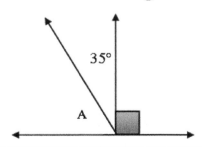

35°

A

Chapter 5

Lesson 6: Finding Area, Volume, & Surface Area

You can scan the QR code given below or use the url to access additional EdSearch resources including videos and mobile apps related to *Finding Area, Volume, & Surface Area.*

ed Search **Finding Area, Volume, & Surface Area**

URL	QR Code
http://www.lumoslearning.com/a/7gb6	

1. **Find the area of the rectangle shown below.**

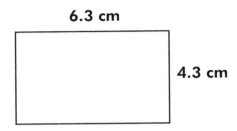

6.3 cm

4.3 cm

Ⓐ 10.5 square centimeters
Ⓑ 24 square centimeters
Ⓒ 27.09 square centimeters
Ⓓ 21 square centimeters

2. **What is the volume of a cube whose sides measure 8 inches?**

Ⓐ 24 in³
Ⓑ 64 in³
Ⓒ 128 in³
Ⓓ 512 in³

3. **Calculate the area of the following polygon.**

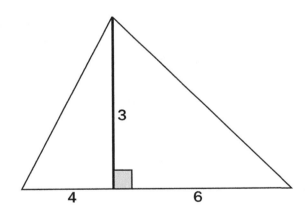

3

4   6

Ⓐ 15 square units
Ⓑ 30 square units
Ⓒ 36 square units
Ⓓ 18 square units

4. Calculate the area of the following polygon.

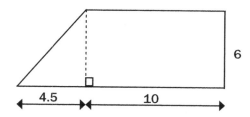

- Ⓐ 60 square units
- Ⓑ 73.5 square units
- Ⓒ 13.5 square units
- Ⓓ 24 square units

5. What is the volume of the following triangular prism?

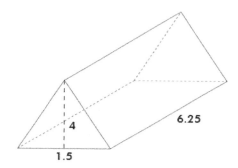

- Ⓐ 11.75 cubic units
- Ⓑ 20 cubic units
- Ⓒ 37.5 cubic units
- Ⓓ 18.75 cubic units

6. What is the volume of a prism with the following base and a height of 2.75?

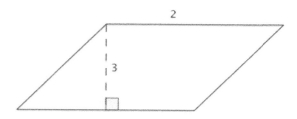

- Ⓐ 8.25 cubic units
- Ⓑ 13.75 cubic units
- Ⓒ 16.5 cubic units
- Ⓓ 8.75 cubic units

7. **What is the surface area of a cube with sides of length 2?**

    Ⓐ 16 square units
    Ⓑ 8 square units
    Ⓒ 24 square units
    Ⓓ 18 square units

8. **What is the surface area of a rectangular prism with dimensions $2, \dfrac{1}{2}$, and $\dfrac{1}{4}$?**

    Ⓐ 2

    Ⓑ $\dfrac{13}{4}$

    Ⓒ $\dfrac{9}{4}$

    Ⓓ $\dfrac{3}{2}$

9. **Find the area of the shape below. (Round to the nearest tenth). Use pi = 3.14.**

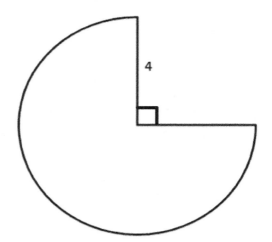

    Ⓐ 37.7 square units
    Ⓑ 50.2 square units
    Ⓒ 18.8 square units
    Ⓓ 35.2 square units

10. John has a container with a volume of 170 cubic feet filled with sand. He wants to transfer his sand into the new container shown below so he can store more sand. After he transfers the sand, how much more sand is remaining in the old container?

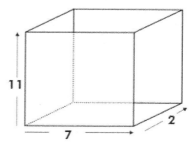

    Ⓐ 16 cubic feet of sand
    Ⓑ 26 cubic feet of sand
    Ⓒ 150 cubic feet of sand
    Ⓓ 324 cubic feet of sand

11. What is the area of the shape? Write your answer in the box given below.

56 in.

123 in.

12. Match the question with the correct type of measurement.

	Area	Surface Area	Volume
How much liquid does this bucket hold?	○	○	○
How much wrapping paper do I need to cover or wrap a box?	○	○	○
How much carpet do I need to cover the floor of this room?	○	○	○

13. Find the volume of a right pyramid that has a height of 14 in. and a base area of 25 in².

Round your answer to the nearest whole number and write the answer in the box.

14. Match the formula to the correct term.

Area of a triangle	●————●	
Volume of a cube	●————●	
Area of rectangle	●————●	

$$\blacksquare\blacksquare\; s^3 \qquad \blacksquare\blacksquare\; l.b \qquad \blacksquare\blacksquare\; \frac{1}{2}.b.h$$

15. What is the volume of a rectangular prism with dimensions 6, $\dfrac{1}{2}$, $\dfrac{1}{4}$ feet?

End of Geometry

Chapter 6:
Statistics and Probability

Lesson 1: Sampling a Population

You can scan the QR code given below or use the url to access additional EdSearch resources including videos and mobile apps related to *Sampling a Population*.

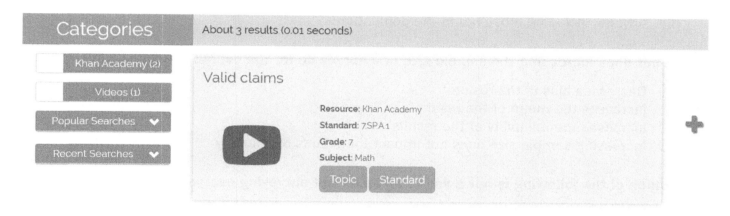

Categories	About 3 results (0.01 seconds)
Khan Academy (2)	**Valid claims**
Videos (1)	
Popular Searches ⌄	**Resource:** Khan Academy
Recent Searches ⌄	**Standard:** 7.SP.A.1
	Grade: 7
	Subject: Math
	Topic Standard

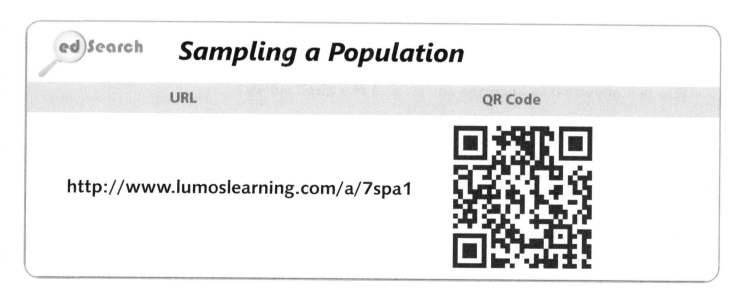

ed Search   *Sampling a Population*

URL	QR Code
http://www.lumoslearning.com/a/7spa1	

1. **Joe and Mary want to calculate the average height of students in their school. Which of the following groups of students would produce the least amount of bias?**

   Ⓐ Every student in the 8th grade.
   Ⓑ Every student on the school basketball team.
   Ⓒ A randomly selected group of students in the halls.
   Ⓓ Joe & Mary's friends.

2. **Which of the following represents who you should survey in a population?**

   Ⓐ A random, representative group from the population
   Ⓑ Every individual in a population
   Ⓒ Only those in the population that agree with you
   Ⓓ Anyone, including those not in the population

3. **What does increasing the sample size of a survey do for the overall results?**

   Ⓐ Decreases bias in the results
   Ⓑ Increases the mean of the results
   Ⓒ Increases the reliability of the results
   Ⓓ Increasing sample size does not impact the results of a survey

4. **Which of the following is not a valid reason for not surveying everyone in a population?**

   Ⓐ It takes a far longer amount of time to survey everyone.
   Ⓑ Not everyone will be willing to participate in the survey.
   Ⓒ It is hard to determine the exact size of a population necessary to ensure everyone is surveyed.
   Ⓓ Surveying everyone produces unreliable results.

5. **Why is it important to know the sample size of a given survey?**

   Ⓐ It helps determine whether any bias exists.
   Ⓑ It helps determine how reliable the results are.
   Ⓒ It gives a good estimate for the size of the target population.
   Ⓓ It is not important to know the sample size.

6. **John and Maggie want to calculate the average height of students in their school. Which of the following groups of students would most likely produce the most amount of bias?**

   Ⓐ Every student in the 8th grade.
   Ⓑ Every student on the school basketball team.
   Ⓒ A randomly selected group of students in the halls.
   Ⓓ John & Maggie's friends.

7. **Which of the following question types will provide the most useful statistical results?**

   Ⓐ Open-ended questions where the person surveyed can answer in any way they want
   Ⓑ Multiple choice questions offering the person a representative number of choices
   Ⓒ True or false questions

8. **Which of the following does not represent a way of avoiding bias in survey results?**

   Ⓐ Use neutral words in the questions asked
   Ⓑ Ensure a random sample of the population
   Ⓒ Only survey individuals that will answer a certain way
   Ⓓ Tailor the conclusions based on survey results, not previous thoughts

9. **The following data set represents survey results on a scale of 1 to 10.**

   {8, 8, 9, 8, 6, 7, 7, 7, 8, 8, 6}

   Which of the following survey result would you be most surprised with if given by the next person surveyed?

   Ⓐ 6
   Ⓑ 5
   Ⓒ 8
   Ⓓ 7

10. **The following data set represents survey results on a scale of 1 to 10.**

    {6, 6, 7, 6, 8, 7, 7, 7, 6, 6, 8}

    Which of the following survey results would you be most surprised with if given by the next person surveyed?

    Ⓐ 6
    Ⓑ 10
    Ⓒ 8
    Ⓓ 7

11. **A company is conducting a survey on their performance with customer service. What method will best avoid receiving biased data?**

    Ⓐ The company should make the survey anonymous.
    Ⓑ The company should take a video survey.
    Ⓒ The company should require the survey during the transaction.
    Ⓓ The company should just request that everyone fill out a survey.

12. **A company is conducting a survey on their performance with customer service. What should the survey look like?**

    Ⓐ The survey should contain a few simple multiple choice questions with an optional comment section.
    Ⓑ The survey should contain simple free response questions with an optional comment section.
    Ⓒ The survey should contain only free response questions.
    Ⓓ The survey should contain some personal questions.

13. **Where should a survey about personal items purchased be conducted?**

    Ⓐ The receipt should have a link to the survey website.
    Ⓑ The survey should be near the register.
    Ⓒ The survey should be near the exit doors.
    Ⓓ The survey should be in the parking lot.

14. **How should online video game surveys be conducted?**

    Ⓐ This survey should be put at the end of a level or section of the game.
    Ⓑ This survey should be put at the beginning of the game.
    Ⓒ Thus survey should be put on flyers and distributed at a gaming store.
    Ⓓ This survey should be put on the website separate from the game.

15. **A large corporation is launching a new product, Hitz, which allows customers to purchase music and store it on the corporation's servers. They want to survey people who listen to a lot of music. Which of the following would give them the best sample?**

    Ⓐ Conducting a survey inside of a music store
    Ⓑ Conducting a survey at the parking lot of a music concert
    Ⓒ Conducting an online survey on music social networking websites
    Ⓓ Conducting a survey of students in a school marching band.

16. Match the situation with the sampling method used.

	Convenience Sample	Systematic Sample	Simple Random Sample
A person chooses every 5th person on a list of names starting with #1.	◯	◯	◯
A person accepts the first 15 people to respond to a magazine ad.	◯	◯	◯
A person picks names out of a hat.	◯	◯	◯

17. A jar of marbles contains gray and black marbles. You collect the representative sample shown here:

if the jar contains 50 marbles, about how many marbles are gray?

Write your answer in the box given below.

Chapter 6

Lesson 2: Describing Multiple Samples

You can scan the QR code given below or use the url to access additional EdSearch resources including videos and mobile apps related to *Describing Multiple Samples*.

ed)Search *Describing Multiple Samples*

URL	QR Code
http://www.lumoslearning.com/a/7spa2	

1. John comes up with the following methods for generating unbiased samples from shoppers at a mall.

   I. Ask random strangers in the mall

   II. Always go to the mall at the same time of day

   III. Go to different places in the mall

   IV. Don't ask questions the same way to different people

   Which of these techniques represents the best way of generating an unbiased sample?

   Ⓐ I and II
   Ⓑ I and III
   Ⓒ I, II, and III
   Ⓓ All of these

2. These two samples are about students' favorite subjects. What inference can you make concerning the students' favorite subjects?

Student samples	Science	Math	English Language Arts	Total
#1	40	14	30	84
#2	43	17	33	93

   Ⓐ Students prefer Science over the other subjects.
   Ⓑ Students prefer Math over the other subjects.
   Ⓒ Students prefer English language arts over the other subjects.
   Ⓓ Students prefer History over the other subjects.

3. These two samples are about students' favorite types of movies. What inference can you make concerning the students' favorite types of movies?

Student samples	Comedy	Action	Drama	Total
#1	35	45	19	99
#2	38	48	22	108

   Ⓐ Students prefer action movies over the other types.
   Ⓑ Students prefer drama over the other types.
   Ⓒ Students prefer comedy over the other types.
   Ⓓ none

4. These two samples are about students' favorite fruits. What inference can you make concerning the students' favorite fruits?

Student samples	Blueberries	Bananas	Strawberries	Total
#1	33	18	44	95
#2	30	20	40	90

Ⓐ Students prefer strawberries over the other fruits.
Ⓑ Students prefer bananas over the other fruits.
Ⓒ Students prefer blueberries over the other fruits.
Ⓓ none

5. Jane and Matt conducted two surveys about students' favorite sports to play. What inference can you make concerning the students' favorite sports?

Student samples	Soccer	Basketball	Tennis	Total
#1	50	145	26	221
#2	56	150	20	226

Ⓐ Most students like basketball over soccer or tennis.
Ⓑ Most students like soccer over basketball or tennis.
Ⓒ Most students like tennis over soccer or basketball.
Ⓓ Most students like track.

6. Paul and Maggie conducted two surveys about students' favorite seasons. What inference can you make concerning the students' favorite seasons?

Student samples	Summer	Fall	Spring	Total
#1	100	128	244	472
#2	98	129	250	477

Ⓐ Most students prefer the Spring season over Summer and Fall.
Ⓑ Students prefer the Summer season.
Ⓒ Students prefer the Fall season.
Ⓓ Students prefer the Winter season.

7. **John and Mark conducted two surveys about students' favorite pizza toppings. What inference can you make concerning the students' favorite pizza toppings?**

Student samples	pineapple	pepperoni	extra cheese	Total
#1	145	237	118	500
#2	150	230	120	500

Ⓐ Most students like pepperoni.
Ⓑ Most students like extra cheese.
Ⓒ Most students like pineapple.
Ⓓ The students like pepperoni over pineapple or extra cheese.

8. **Jon and Minny conducted two surveys about students' favorite board games. What inference can you make concerning the students' favorite board games?**

Student samples	Game X	Game Y	Game Z	Total
#1	45	5	6	56
#2	50	6	2	58

Ⓐ Most students like Game Z.
Ⓑ Most students like **Game X** over **Game Y** or Game Z.
Ⓒ Most students like **Game Y**.
Ⓓ Most students don't like **Game X**.

9. **Tom and Bob conducted two surveys about their co-workers' favorite hobbies. What inference can you make concerning their co-workers' favorite hobbies?**

Co-worker sample	Play Golf	Play Video Games	Fishing	Total
#1	125	80	126	331
#2	118	83	130	331

Ⓐ Most of their coworkers spend a lot of money.
Ⓑ Most of their coworkers spend a lot of time inside.
Ⓒ Most of their coworkers spend a lot of time outside.
Ⓓ Most of their coworkers live in big houses.

10. Bill and Jill conducted two surveys about students' favorite card games. What inference can you make concerning the students' favorite card games?

Student samples	Hearts	Go fish	Spades	Total
#1	14	90	11	115
#2	10	88	14	122

Ⓐ Most students like speed.
Ⓑ Most students like hearts.
Ⓒ Most students like spades.
Ⓓ Most students like Go fish over hearts or spades.

11. Moe and Lonnie conducted two surveys about students' favorite soda flavor. What inference can you make concerning the students' favorite soda flavor?

Student samples	Strawberry	Orange	Rootbeer	Total
#1	10	11	88	109
#2	14	14	90	118

Ⓐ Most students like strawberry.
Ⓑ Most students like orange.
Ⓒ Most students like rootbeer over strawberry or orange.
Ⓓ Most students like chocolate.

12. Billy and Larry conducted two surveys about students' favorite subject. What inference can you make concerning the students' favorite subject?

Student samples	Math	English Language Arts	Science	Total
#1	111	111	111	333
#2	114	114	114	342

Ⓐ Most students like science.
Ⓑ Most students like math.
Ⓒ The same number of students like the three subjects equally.
Ⓓ Most students like English Language Arts.

13. Tom and Jerry conducted two surveys about students' favorite ice cream flavor. What inference can you make concerning the students' favorite ice cream flavor?

Student samples	Chocolate	Strawberry	Cookies-n-Cream	Total
#1	59	3	12	74
#2	61	4	15	80

Ⓐ   Most students' like cookies-n-cream.
Ⓑ   Most students like chocolate over strawberry or cookies-n-cream.
Ⓒ   Most students' like strawberry.
Ⓓ   Most students' like strawberry and cookies-n-cream.

14. Paul and Maggie conducted two surveys about students' favorite holiday. What inference can you make concerning the students' favorite holiday?

Student samples	Christmas	Thanksgiving	Easter	Total
#1	100	128	244	472
#2	98	129	250	477

Ⓐ   Most students like Halloween.
Ⓑ   Most students like Christmas.
Ⓒ   Most students like Thanksgiving.
Ⓓ   The students like Easter over Christmas or Thanksgiving.

15. Harper wants to conduct two surveys at his school, where 1,600 students attend. For the first survey, he wants to find out what types of cell phones the students in his school use. Of those students, he wants to survey them to determine their favorite apps. Which of the following is the best method for selecting a random sample?

Ⓐ   Select 20 students from each first period class.
Ⓑ   Select random students as they enter or exit school.
Ⓒ   Select students based on how many text messages they make each month.
Ⓓ   Select all of the students.

16. You want to take a survey of 250 people in the mall in one day. You want to create a simple random sample of 100 people. Which method is most likely to result in a simple random sample?

Circle the correct answer choice.

Ⓐ   Assign each person a number, then select every prime number.
Ⓑ   Select the first 100 people to complete the survey.
Ⓒ   Assign each person a number, then select 100 random numbers.
Ⓓ   Select 100 people close to the bookstore.

17. Your school is thinking about starting a drama club but they want to know if students like the idea. To sample the population, the principal is going to survey every 10th student that walks into the school on Monday morning starting with the first student.

Circle the method of sampling this describes.

Ⓐ Simple Random Sampling
Ⓑ Systematic Sampling
Ⓒ Convenience Sampling

Chapter 6

Lesson 3: Mean, Median, and Mean Absolute Deviation

You can scan the QR code given below or use the url to access additional EdSearch resources including videos and mobile apps related to *Mean, Median, and Mean Absolute Deviation.*

ed)Search ***Mean, Median, and Mean Absolute Deviation***

URL	QR Code
http://www.lumoslearning.com/a/7spb3	

1. **Consider the following dot-plot for Height versus Weight.**

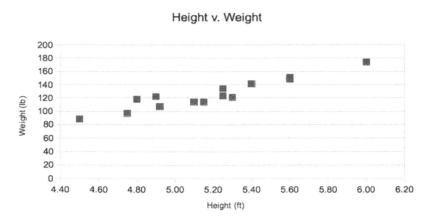

   Height v. Weight

   What does this dot-plot indicate about the correlation between height and weight?

   Ⓐ There is no correlation.
   Ⓑ There is a strong negative correlation.
   Ⓒ There is a strong positive correlation.
   Ⓓ There is a weak positive correlation.

2. **The following chart represents the heights of boys on the basketball and soccer teams.**

Basketball	Soccer
5'4''	4'11''
5'2''	4'10''
5'3''	5'9''
5'5''	5'1''
5'5''	5'0''
5'1''	5'1''
5'9''	5'3''
5'3''	5'1''

   What inference can be made based on this information?

   Ⓐ Soccer players have a higher average skill level than basketball players.
   Ⓑ Soccer players have a lower average weight than basketball players.
   Ⓒ Basketball players have a higher average height than soccer players.
   Ⓓ No inference can be made.

3. Use the table below to answer the question that follows:

Month	Avg Temp.
January	24°F
February	36°F
March	55°F
April	65°F
May	72°F
June	78°F

What is the difference between the mean temperature of the first four months of the year and the mean temperature of the next two months?

Ⓐ 15 degrees
Ⓑ 20 degrees
Ⓒ 25 degrees
Ⓓ 30 degrees

4. Use the table below to answer the question:

Month	Avg Temp.
January	24°F
February	36°F
March	55°F
April	65°F
May	72°F
June	78°F

If the temperature in January was 54°F instead of 24°F, by how much would the mean temperature for the six months increase?

Ⓐ 5°F
Ⓑ 10°F
Ⓒ 30°F
Ⓓ 35°F

5. **Use the table to answer the question below:**

Team	Wins
Mustangs	14
Spartans	17
North Stars	16
Hornets	9
Stallions	13
Renegades	9
Rangers	5

What is the mode of the wins for all the teams in the above table?

Ⓐ 14
Ⓑ 5
Ⓒ 13
Ⓓ 9

6. **Jack scored 7, 9, 2, 6, 15 and 15 points in 6 basketball games. Find the mean, median and mode scores for all the games.**

Ⓐ Mean = 7, Median = 9 and Mode = 2
Ⓑ Mean = 9, Median = 7 and Mode = 15
Ⓒ Mean = 9, Median = 8 and Mode = 15
Ⓓ Mean = 7, Median = 2 and Mode = 9

7. **Mean absolute deviation is a measure of...**

Ⓐ Central Tendency
Ⓑ Variability
Ⓒ Averages
Ⓓ Sample Size

8. Calculate the mean for the following set of data:

$$\left\{ \frac{7}{4}, \frac{3}{4}, \frac{5}{4}, \frac{7}{4}, \frac{3}{4}, \frac{5}{4} \right\}$$

(A) $\dfrac{7}{4}$

(B) $\dfrac{5}{2}$

(C) $\dfrac{5}{4}$

(D) $\dfrac{1}{6}$

9. Another word for mean is...

(A) Average
(B) Middle
(C) Most
(D) Count

10. What is the median for the following set of data?

$$\left\{ \frac{4}{5}, \frac{1}{3}, \frac{1}{3}, \frac{1}{5}, \frac{2}{3} \right\}$$

(A) $\dfrac{1}{3}$

(B) $\dfrac{2}{3}$

(C) $\dfrac{1}{5}$

(D) $\dfrac{1}{4}$

11. What is the mode of the following set of data?

{1, 1, 2, 3, 1, 4, 6, 2, 3}

Ⓐ 2
Ⓑ 3.75
Ⓒ 1
Ⓓ 6

12. John scored 6, 8, 1, 5, 11, 14 and 14 points in 7 lacrosse games. Find the mean, median and mode scores for all the games. (Round to the nearest tenth)

Ⓐ Mean = 8.4, Median = 8 and Mode = 14
Ⓑ Mean = 8.1, Median = 6, and Mode = 14
Ⓒ Mean = 9.3, Median = 8 and Mode = 15
Ⓓ Mean = 7.5, Median = 2 and Mode = 9

13. Calculate the mean for the following set of data:

{ 0.3, 1.2, 2.5, 4.3 }

Round your answer to the nearest tenth.

Ⓐ 2.1
Ⓑ 2.7
Ⓒ 8.3
Ⓓ 2.5

14. Calculate the median for the following set of data:

{ 0.3, 1.2, 2.5, 4.3 }

Round your answer to the nearest tenth.

Ⓐ 1.8
Ⓑ 2.1
Ⓒ 1.9
Ⓓ 1.2

15. What is the mean absolute deviation for the following set of data?

{2, 5, 7, 1, 2}

Ⓐ 3.4
Ⓑ 2
Ⓒ 2.08
Ⓓ 5

16. Fill in the blanks in the table with the correct value of mean or median. Round the number to the tenth place in case the answer is not a whole number.

	Median	Mean
Data Set : 9, 8, 7, 4, 5		6.6
Data Set : 5, 8, 5, 9, 1, 2	5	
Data Set : 1, 2, 8, 1, 3, 3		3

17. The mean of a data set is 5. The minimum of the data is 2. What is the deviation of the minimum?

Write your answer in the box given below.

Chapter 6

Lesson 4: Mean, Median, and Mode

You can scan the QR code given below or use the url to access additional EdSearch resources including videos and mobile apps related to *Mean, Median, and Mode.*

ed)Search *Mean, Median, and Mode*

URL	QR Code
http://www.lumoslearning.com/a/7spb4	

1. The following data set represents a score from 1-10 for a customers' experience at a local restaurant.

   { 1, 1, 2, 1, 3, 4, 7, 8, 1, 3, 4, 2, 1, 3, 7, 2 }

   If a score of 1 means the customer did not have a good experience, and a 10 means the customer had a fantastic experience, what can you infer by looking at the data?

   Ⓐ Overall, customers had a good experience.
   Ⓑ Overall, customers had a bad experience.
   Ⓒ Overall, customers had an "ok" experience.
   Ⓓ Nothing can be inferred from this data.

2. The manager of a local pizza place has asked you to make suggestions on how to improve his menu. The following bar graph represents the results of a survey asking customers what their favorite food at the restaurant was.

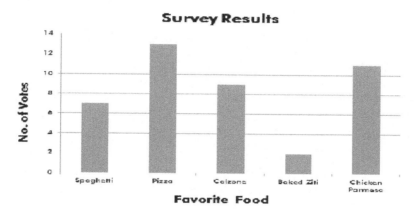

   Based on these survey results, which menu item would you suggest the manager remove from the menu?

   Ⓐ Spaghetti
   Ⓑ Pizza
   Ⓒ Calzone
   Ⓓ Baked Ziti

3. What are the measures of central tendency?

   Ⓐ Mean, Median, Mode
   Ⓑ Median, Mode, Mean Absolute Deviation
   Ⓒ Median, Mean Absolute Deviation, Sample Size
   Ⓓ Mean, Median, Range

4. **What is the mean absolute deviation for the following set of data?**

    {1, 2, 3, 4}

    Ⓐ 1
    Ⓑ 2.5
    Ⓒ 4
    Ⓓ 2

5. **What are the central tendencies of the following data set? (round to the nearest tenth)**

    {2, 2, 3, 4, 6, 8, 9, 10, 13, 13, 16, 17}

    Ⓐ Mean: 8.6, Median: 8.5, Mode: 2, 13
    Ⓑ Mean: 8.5, Median: 8.4, Mode: 2, 3
    Ⓒ Mean: 8.5, Median: 8.6, Mode: 2, 13
    Ⓓ Mean: 7.6, Median: 7.5, Mode: 10, 13

6. **What are the central tendencies of the following data set? (round to the nearest tenth)**

    {11, 11, 12, 13, 15, 17, 18, 20, 23, 23, 26, 27}

    Ⓐ Mean: 17.2, Median: 17.5, Mode: none
    Ⓑ Mean: 18.5, Median: 16, Mode: 11
    Ⓒ Mean: 17.5, Median: 18, Mode: 23
    Ⓓ Mean: 18, Median: 17.5, Mode: 11, 23

7. **What are the central tendencies of the following data set? (round to the nearest tenth)**

    {31, 31, 32, 33, 35, 37, 38, 41, 54, 54, 57, 58}

    Ⓐ Mean: 41.4, Median: 37.5, Mode: 31
    Ⓑ Mean: 41.5, Median: 36.5, Mode: none
    Ⓒ Mean: 41.6, Median: 38.5, Mode: 31, 54
    Ⓓ Mean: 41.8, Median: 37.5, Mode: 31, 54

8. **What are the central tendencies of the following data set? (round to the nearest tenth)**

    {41, 41, 42, 43, 45, 47, 48, 51, 64, 64, 64, 67}

    Ⓐ Mean: 51.4, Median: 47.5, Mode: 64
    Ⓑ Mean: 48.5, Median: 46, Mode: 64
    Ⓒ Mean: 47.5, Median: 48, Mode: 64
    Ⓓ Mean: 47, Median: 47.5, Mode: 64

9. **What are the central tendencies of the following data set? (round to the nearest tenth)**

{51, 51, 52, 53, 55, 57, 58, 61, 54, 54, 57, 54}

Ⓐ Mean: 58.5, Median: 56, Mode: 54
Ⓑ Mean: 54.8, Median: 54, Mode: 54
Ⓒ Mean: 57.5, Median: 58, Mode: 54
Ⓓ Mean: 57.6, Median: 57.5, Mode: 54

10. **What are the central tendencies of the following data set? (round to the nearest tenth)**

{61, 61, 52, 53, 65, 67, 58, 61, 64, 64, 57, 54}

Ⓐ Mean: 59.8, Median: 61, Mode: 61
Ⓑ Mean: 58.5, Median: 66, Mode: 64
Ⓒ Mean: 57.5, Median: 68, Mode: 64
Ⓓ Mean: 57.9, Median: 67.5, Mode: 64

11. **What are the central tendencies of the following data set? (round to the nearest tenth)**

{71, 71, 62, 63, 75, 77, 68, 71, 74, 74, 67, 74}

Ⓐ Mean: 70.6, Median: 78, Mode: 74
Ⓑ Mean: 68.5, Median: 76, Mode: 74
Ⓒ Mean: 70.6, Median: 71, Mode: 71, 74
Ⓓ Mean: 77, Median: 77.5, Mode: 74

12. **What are the central tendencies of the following data set? (round to the nearest tenth)**

{61, 71, 52, 63, 65, 77, 58, 71, 64, 74, 57, 74}

Ⓐ Mean: 65.6, Median: 64.5, Mode: 71, 74
Ⓑ Mean: 68.5, Median: 66, Mode: none
Ⓒ Mean: 67.5, Median: 68, Mode: 71
Ⓓ Mean: 67, Median: 67.5, Mode: 2

13. **What are the central tendencies of the following data set? (round to the nearest tenth)**

{21, 21, 22, 23, 35, 37, 38, 41, 44, 44, 47, 44}

Ⓐ Mean: 38.5, Median: 37.5, Mode: 44
Ⓑ Mean: 34.8, Median: 37.5, Mode: 44
Ⓒ Mean: 37.5, Median: 38, Mode: none
Ⓓ Mean: 37, Median: 37.5, Mode: 54

14. Kelli's Ice Cream Shop must have a mean of 110 visitors per day in order to make a profit. The table below shows the number of visitors during one week.

	No of Visitors
Sunday	63
Monday	77
Tuesday	121
Wednesday	96
Thursday	137
Friday	154

Based on the table, how many visitors will need to go to Kelli's Ice Cream shop on Saturday in order for the company to make a profit for the week?

Ⓐ 108
Ⓑ 110
Ⓒ 122
Ⓓ 222

15. Henry made a list of his math scores for one grading period: 98, 87, 93, 89, 90, 85, 88. If Henry adds a 90 to the list to represent his final test for the grading period, which statement is true?

Ⓐ The mode would decrease.
Ⓑ The mean would increase.
Ⓒ The median would increase.
Ⓓ The mean would decrease.

16. Calculate the Mean, Median and Mode for the data set given below.

5, 5, 9, 4, 6, 7

Match the value of the answer to it's correct category.

	Mean	Median	Mode
6	○	○	○
5.5	○	○	○
5	○	○	○

17. Find the interquartile range of the data set.

32.6, 98.5, 16.6, 22.4, 99.8, 72.6, 68.2, 51.8, and 49.3.

Chapter 6

Lesson 5: Understanding Probability

You can scan the QR code given below or use the url to access additional EdSearch resources including videos and mobile apps related to *Understanding Probability*.

 *Understanding Probability*

URL	QR Code
http://www.lumoslearning.com/a/7spc5	

1. Mary has 3 red marbles and 7 yellow marbles in a bag. If she were to remove 2 red and 1 yellow marbles and set them aside, what is the probability of her pulling a yellow marble as her next marble?

   Ⓐ $\dfrac{1}{6}$

   Ⓑ $\dfrac{1}{7}$

   Ⓒ $\dfrac{7}{10}$

   Ⓓ $\dfrac{6}{7}$

2. John has a deck of cards (52 cards). If John removes a number 2 card from the deck, what is the probability that he will pick a number 2 card at random?

   Ⓐ 3 out of 51
   Ⓑ 4 out of 51
   Ⓒ 26 out of 51
   Ⓓ 30 out of 51

3. Maggie has a bag of coins (8 nickels, 6 quarters, 12 dimes, 20 pennies). If she picks a coin at random, what is the probability that she will pick a quarter?

   Ⓐ 2 out of 15
   Ⓑ 3 out of 23
   Ⓒ 3 out of 50
   Ⓓ 5 out of 46

4. Mark has a box of bills (12 ones, 8 tens, 21 twenties, 30 fifties). If he picks a bill at random, what is the probability that he will pick a ten?

   Ⓐ 8 out of 71
   Ⓑ 8 out of 100
   Ⓒ 10 out of 71
   Ⓓ 7 out of 71

5. Moe has a bowl of nuts (14 pecans, 8 walnuts, 28 almonds, 33 peanuts). If he picks a nut at random, what is the probability that he will pick a peanut?

   Ⓐ 33 out of 70
   Ⓑ 33 out of 80
   Ⓒ 33 out of 100
   Ⓓ 33 out of 83

6. Xavier has a bowl of nuts (14 pecans, 8 walnuts, 28 almonds, 33 peanuts). If he picks out all the pecans, what is the probability that he will pick a walnut at random?

   Ⓐ 8 out of 83
   Ⓑ 8 out of 69
   Ⓒ 8 out of 100
   Ⓓ 8 out of 70

7. Tim has a box of chocolates with the following flavors: 24 cherry, 26 caramel, 20 fudge, and 16 candy. If he picks out two of each type of chocolate, what is the probability that he will pick a cherry chocolate at random?

   Ⓐ 11 out of 35
   Ⓑ 4 out of 13
   Ⓒ 11 out of 50
   Ⓓ 11 out of 39

8. Clarissa has a box of chocolates with the following flavors: 24 cherry, 26 caramel, 20 fudge, and 16 taffy. If she picks out all the taffy, what is the probability that she will pick a fudge chocolate at random?

   Ⓐ 2 out of 7
   Ⓑ 10 out of 43
   Ⓒ 1 out of 5
   Ⓓ 8 out of 35

9. Karen has a box of chocolates with the following flavors: 24 cherry, 26 caramel, 20 fudge, and 16 taffy. If she removes half of the cherry and fudge chocolates from the box, what is the probability that she will pick a taffy chocolate at random?

   Ⓐ 1 out of 4
   Ⓑ 8 out of 43
   Ⓒ 4 out of 25
   Ⓓ 16 out of 43

10. The table below shows the types of fruits Jessie's mom purchased from the grocery store.

Type of Fruit	Number of Fruits
Apple	6
Orange	4
Pear	2
Peaches	3

If Jessie grabs one of the fruits without looking, what is the probability that he will NOT pick a peach?

Ⓐ $\dfrac{2}{5}$

Ⓑ $\dfrac{3}{15}$

Ⓒ $\dfrac{4}{5}$

Ⓓ $\dfrac{2}{3}$

11. The table shows the types of books five friends like. One friend is chosen at random. Identify the outcome of the event. Event: The friend that likes non-fiction.

Circle the outcome of the event shown below.

Favorite Types of Books

Ⓐ Friend - Type
Ⓑ Sarah - Fiction
Ⓒ John - Non-Fiction
Ⓓ Billy - Fantasy
Ⓔ Raj - Mystery
Ⓕ Kavi - Romance

12. When one number cube is rolled, the following six outcomes are possible.

   Identify the outcomes for each event.

   Fill in the blanks given in the table with the correct outcomes.

Event	Outcome
The number cube comes up odd.	1, 3, 5
The number cube comes up even.	
The number cube comes up greater than 3.	
The number cube comes up less than or equal to 5.	

Chapter 6

Lesson 6: Predicting Using Probability

You can scan the QR code given below or use the url to access additional EdSearch resources including videos and mobile apps related to *Predicting Using Probability*.

 **Search** *Predicting Using Probability*

URL	QR Code
http://www.lumoslearning.com/a/7spc6	

1. **Which of the following represents the sample space for flipping two coins?**

   Ⓐ {HH, TT}
   Ⓑ {H, T}
   Ⓒ {HH, HT, TH, TT}
   Ⓓ {HH, HT, TT}

2. **Which of the following experiments would best test the statement, "The probability of a coin landing on heads is 1/2."?**

   Ⓐ Toss a coin 1,000 times, and record the results.
   Ⓑ Toss a coin twice to see if it lands on heads one out of those two times.
   Ⓒ Toss a coin until it lands on heads and record the number of tries it took.
   Ⓓ Toss a coin twice, if it doesn't land on heads exactly once, the theoretical probability is false.

3. **Which of the following results is most likely from rolling a six-sided die?**

   Ⓐ Rolling an odd number
   Ⓑ Rolling an even number
   Ⓒ Rolling a number from 1 to 3
   Ⓓ All of the above are equally likely.

4. **Sandy flipped a coin 40 times. Her results are 75% heads and 25% tails. What is the difference between the actual results and the expected results?**

   Ⓐ 20%
   Ⓑ 50%
   Ⓒ 25%
   Ⓓ 10%

5. **Maggie rolled a pair of four sided dice 10 times. The results are 30% side 1, 20% side 2, 20% side 3, 30% side 4. What is the difference between the results and the expected results for all four sides?**

Ⓐ 25% side 1,
    25% side 2,
    25% side 3,
    25% side 4

Ⓑ 5% side 1,
    5% side 2,
    5% side 3,
    5% side 4

Ⓒ 5% side 1,
    25% side 2,
    25% side 3,
    5% side 4

Ⓓ 4% side 1,
    4% side 2,
    4% side 3,
    4% side 4

6. **Maggie rolls two pairs of four sided dice 10 times. The results were 30% side 1, 20% side 2, 20% side 3, 30% side 4. What were the actual results and expected results?**

Ⓐ Results: 12 side 1, 8 side 2, 8 side 3, 12 side 4 ...Expected Results: 10 side 1, 10 side 2, 10 side 3, 10 side 4
Ⓑ Results: 6 side 1, 4 side 2, 4 side 3, 6 side 4 ...Expected Results: 5 side 1, 5 side 2, 5 side 3, 5 side 4
Ⓒ Results: 6 side 1, 4 side 2, 4 side 3, 6 side 4 ...Expected Results: 10 side 1, 10 side 2, 10 side 3, 10 side 4
Ⓓ Results: 10 side 1, 10 side 2, 10 side 3, 10 side 4 ...Expected Results: 12 side 1, 8 side 2, 8 side 3, 12 side 4

7. **Juliana was expected to make 80% of her first serves in the tennis match. She made half of 60 first serves in the match. What were the results and expected results?**

Ⓐ Results: 30 first serves. Expected Results: 48 first serves
Ⓑ Results: 20 first serves. Expected Results: 48 first serves
Ⓒ Results: 25 first serves. Expected Results: 48 first serves
Ⓓ Results: 35 first serves. Expected Results: 48 first serves

8. **Which of the following represents the sample space for rolling a pair of four-sided dice?**

    Ⓐ (1,1) (1,2) (1,3) (1,4) (2,2) (2,3) (2,4) (3,3) (3,4) (4,4)
    Ⓑ (1,2) (1,3) (1,4) (2,3) (2,4) (3,4)
    Ⓒ (1,2) (1,3) (1,4) (2,3) (2,4)(3,4) (4,4)
    Ⓓ (1,2) (1,3) (1,4) (2,3) (2,4)

9. **Lea is playing a carnival game and has a chance to win a large stuffed teddy bear. In order to win, she has to guess the color of cube she will pick out of a box. The box is shown below.**

    "Pick the Cube" Carnival Game

    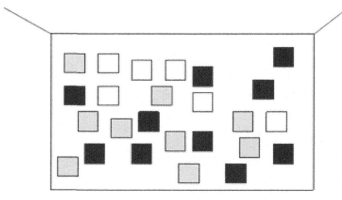

    Based on the colors and number of blocks, what is Lea's chance of winning the game if she says that she will pick a black cube out of the box?

    Ⓐ 60%
    Ⓑ 10%
    Ⓒ 90%
    Ⓓ 40%

10. **Ms. Green is passing out snacks during her tutoring session. She has 7 bags of chips, 13 candy bars, 16 fruit snacks, and 10 lollipops. If one of Ms. Green's students randomly selects a snack, what is the probability that he will select a fruit snack? Round your answer to the nearest tenth of a percent.**

    Ⓐ 34.8%
    Ⓑ 65.2%
    Ⓒ 16.0%
    Ⓓ 84.0%

11. Mark the correct probabilities for each event.

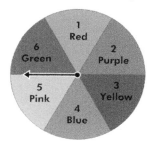

	$\frac{1}{6}$	$\frac{1}{3}$	$\frac{1}{2}$
The probability you spin an odd number.	○	○	○
The probability you spin a 3.	○	○	○
The probability you spin a blue.	○	○	○
The probability you spin a red or yellow.	○	○	○

12. What is the probability that the spinner will stop on the #3 sector?

Circle the correct answer choice.

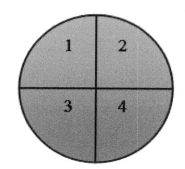

Ⓐ 1.3

Ⓑ $\frac{1}{2}$

Ⓒ $\frac{1}{3}$

Ⓓ $\frac{1}{4}$

Chapter 6

Lesson 7: Using Probability Models

You can scan the QR code given below or use the url to access additional EdSearch resources including videos and mobile apps related to *Using Probability Models*.

 **Using Probability Models**

URL	QR Code
http://www.lumoslearning.com/a/7spc7a	

1. Sara rolls two dice, one black and one yellow. What is the probability that she will roll a 3 on the black die and a 5 on the yellow die?

   (A) $\dfrac{1}{6}$

   (B) $\dfrac{1}{12}$

   (C) $\dfrac{2}{15}$

   (D) $\dfrac{1}{36}$

2. Which of the following represents the probability of an event most likely to occur?

   (A) 0.25
   (B) 0.91
   (C) 0.58
   (D) 0.15

3. Which of the following is not a valid probability?

   (A) 0.25

   (B) $\dfrac{1}{5}$

   (C) 1

   (D) $\dfrac{5}{4}$

4. Tom tosses a coin 12 times. The coin lands on heads only twice. If Tom tosses the coin one more time, what is the probability that the coin will land on heads?

   (A) 40%
   (B) 50%
   (C) 60%
   (D) 15%

5. Joe has 5 nickels, 5 dimes, 5 quarters, and 5 pennies in his pocket. Six times, he randomly picked a coin from his pocket and put it back. Joe picked a dime every time. If he randomly picks a coin from his pocket again, what is the probability the coin will be a dime?

   Ⓐ 33%
   Ⓑ 100%
   Ⓒ 24%
   Ⓓ 25%

6. Jim rolls a pair of six-sided dice five times. He rolls a pair of two's five times in a row. If he rolls the dice one more time, what is the probability he will roll a pair of fours?

   Ⓐ 1 out of 21
   Ⓑ 1 out of 36
   Ⓒ 1 out of 24
   Ⓓ 1 out of 6

7. Bob rolls a six-sided die and flips a coin five times. He rolls a three and flips the coin to tails five times in a row. If he rolls the die and flips the coin one more time, what is the probability he will roll a three and flip the coin on tails?

   Ⓐ 1 out of 6
   Ⓑ 1 out of 10
   Ⓒ 1 out of 12
   Ⓓ 1 out of 7

8. Mia rolls a pair of six-sided dice and flips two coins ten times. She rolls a pair of threes and flips the coins to tails ten times in a row. If she rolls the dice and flips the coins one more time, what is the probability she will roll all fives and flip the coins on heads?

   Ⓐ 1 out of 60
   Ⓑ 1 out of 144
   Ⓒ 1 out of 128
   Ⓓ 1 out of 64

9. Sophia wants to select a pair of shorts from Too Sweet Clothing Store. The store has 2 different colors of shorts (black (B) and green (G)) available in sizes of small (S), medium (M), and large (L). If Sophia grabs a pair of shorts without looking, which sample space shows the different types of shorts she could select?

   Ⓐ {BS, BM, BL, GS, GM, GL}
   Ⓑ {BB, BG, SS, SM, SL}
   Ⓒ {BG, SM, SL}
   Ⓓ {BS, BL, GS, GL}

10. Eric's Pizza Shop is offering a sale on any large two-topping pizza for $8.00. Customers have a choice between thin crust (T) or pan pizza (Z), one meat topping [pepperoni(P), Italian sausage (I), or ham (H)], and one vegetable topping [green peppers (G), onions (O), or mushrooms (M)]. Which sample space shows the number of possible combinations customers can have if they select a thin crust pizza?

Ⓐ {TPG, TIO, THM}
Ⓑ {TPG, TPO, TPM, TIG, TIO, TIM, THG, THO, THM}
Ⓒ {TPG, TPO, TIG, TIO, THG, THO}
Ⓓ {TPG, TPO, TPM, TIG, TIO, TIM, THG, THO, THM, PPG, PPO, PPM, PIG, PIO, PIM, PHG, PHO, PHM}

11. There is a bag of tiles with 5 black tiles, 5 white tiles, and 5 blue tiles. You are going to choose one tile at random. Are the outcomes of this event equally likely?

Circle the correct answer.

Ⓐ Yes

Ⓑ No

12. You are playing a game using this spinner. You get one spin on each turn. Which list shows a complete probability model for the spinner?

Circle the correct answer.

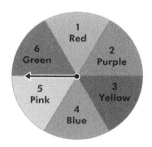

Ⓐ P(even number) = $\frac{3}{6}$, P(odd number) = $\frac{3}{6}$

Ⓑ P(red) = $\frac{1}{6}$, P(blue) = $\frac{1}{6}$

Ⓒ P(number <4) = $\frac{3}{6}$

Ⓓ P(yellow or green) = $\frac{2}{6}$, P(red or blue) = $\frac{2}{6}$

Chapter 6

Lesson 8: Probability Models from Observed Frequencies

You can scan the QR code given below or use the url to access additional EdSearch resources including videos and mobile apps related to *Probability Models from Observed Frequencies.*

ed)Search *Probability Models from Observed Frequencies*

URL	QR Code
http://www.lumoslearning.com/a/7spc7b	

1. Felix flipped a coin 8 times and got the following results: H, H, T, H, H, T, T, H. If these results were typical for that coin, what are the odds of flipping a heads with that coin?

   Ⓐ 3 out of 5
   Ⓑ 5 out of 8
   Ⓒ 3 out of 8
   Ⓓ 1 out of 2

2. Bridgette rolled a six-sided die 100 times to test the frequency of each number's appearing. According to these statistics, how many times should a 2 be rolled out of 50 rolls?

Number	Frequency
1	18%
2	20%
3	16%
4	11%
5	18%
6	17%

   Ⓐ 10 times
   Ⓑ 20 times
   Ⓒ 12 times
   Ⓓ 15 times

3. Randomly choosing a number out of a hat 50 times resulted in choosing an odd number a total of four more times than the number of times an even number was chosen. How many times was an even number chosen from the hat?

   Ⓐ 27 times
   Ⓑ 21 times
   Ⓒ 29 times
   Ⓓ 23 times

4. 8 out of the last 12 customers at Paul's Pizza ordered pepperoni pizza. According to this data, what is the probability that the next customer will NOT order pepperoni pizza?

   Ⓐ 1 out of 3
   Ⓑ 4 out of 5
   Ⓒ 1 out of 2
   Ⓓ 2 out of 5

5. Susan is selling cookies for a fundraiser. Out of the last 20 people she asked, 10 people bought 1 box of cookies, 5 bought more than 1 box, and 5 bought none. Based on this data, what is the probability that the next person she asks will buy at least 1 box of cookies?

    Ⓐ 1 out of 3
    Ⓑ 2 out of 5
    Ⓒ 4 out of 5
    Ⓓ 3 out of 4

6. William has passed 9 out of his last 10 tests in Spanish class. Based on his past history, what is the probability that he will NOT pass the next test?

    Ⓐ 10%
    Ⓑ 25%
    Ⓒ 15%
    Ⓓ 8%

7. Travis has scored goals in 7 of his last 9 soccer games. At this rate, what is the probability that he will score in his next game? Round the nearest percent.

    Ⓐ 70%
    Ⓑ 17%
    Ⓒ 78%
    Ⓓ 53%

8. Gabe's free throw percentage for the season has been 80%. Based on this, if he has 5 free throws in the next game, how many is he likely to miss?

    Ⓐ 0
    Ⓑ 1
    Ⓒ 2
    Ⓓ 3

9. York and his partner have won the doubles tennis tournament three out of the last four years. According to this record, what is the probability they will win it again this year?

    Ⓐ 3 out of 4
    Ⓑ 1 out of 3
    Ⓒ 1 out of 2
    Ⓓ 4 out of 5

10. Robbie runs track. His finishes for his last 6 events were: 1st, 3rd, 2nd, 5th, 4th, 2nd. Based on these results, what is the probability he will finish in the top 3 of his next event?

Ⓐ 4 out of 5
Ⓑ 2 out of 3
Ⓒ 1 out of 2
Ⓓ 3 out of 4

11. The table shows observed frequencies of spinning a spinner with 4 numbers on it (1, 2, 3, 4).

	Experiment Table				
Outcome	1	2	3	4	50 total trials
Frequency	6	11	19	14	

What is the observed probability of spinning a 4?

Circle the correct answer choice.

Ⓐ $P(4) = \dfrac{2}{7}$

Ⓑ $P(4) = 14$

Ⓒ $P(4) = \dfrac{4}{14}$

Ⓓ $P(4) = \dfrac{7}{25}$

12. The table shows observed frequencies of rolling a six sided dice. Mark the probabilities of different outcomes given in the table.

	Experiment Table					
Outcome	1	2	3	4	5	6	50 total trials
Frequency	7	9	10	8	9	7	

	$\dfrac{24}{50}$	$\dfrac{26}{50}$
Probability of rolling greater than or equal to 4	○	○
Probability of rolling less than 4	○	○
Probability of rolling an even number	○	○
Probability of rolling an odd number	○	○

Chapter 6

Lesson 9: Find the Probability of a Compound Event

You can scan the QR code given below or use the url to access additional EdSearch resources including videos and mobile apps related to *Find the Probability of a Compound Event.*

ed Search *Find the Probability of a Compound Event*

URL	QR Code
http://www.lumoslearning.com/a/7spc7b	

1. The following tree diagram represents Jane's possible outfits:

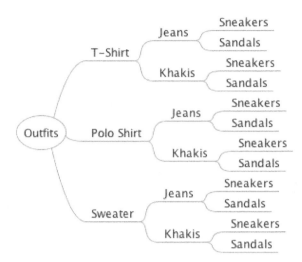

How many different outfits can Jane make based on this diagram?

Ⓐ 2
Ⓑ 12
Ⓒ 16
Ⓓ 4

2. The following tree diagram represents Jane's possible outfits:

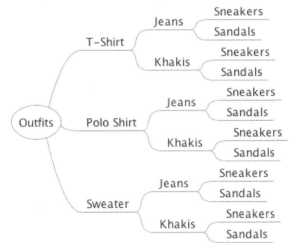

If Jane randomly selects an outfit, what is the probability she will be wearing Jeans AND Sneakers?

(A) $\dfrac{1}{12}$

(B) $\dfrac{1}{3}$

(C) $\dfrac{1}{4}$

(D) $\dfrac{1}{2}$

3. **Paul, Jack, Tom, Fred, and Sam are competing in the long jump. If they win the top five spots, how many ways could they be arranged in the top five spots?**

   (A) 15 ways
   (B) 60 ways
   (C) 120 ways
   (D) 3,125 ways

4. **Mona is about to roll a pair of four-sided dice. What is the probability she will roll a one and a two or a one and a three?**

   (A) 1 out of 8
   (B) 1 out of 16
   (C) 1 out of 12
   (D) 1 out of 4

5. **Tim rolls a pair of six-sided dice. What is the probability he will roll doubles?**

   (A) 6 out of 21
   (B) 1 out of 6
   (C) 1 out of 4
   (D) 2 out of 21

6. The triple jump competition is close. Joe, Damon, Sam, and Chris have a shot at first place. If two of the four tie for first place and the other two tie for second place, how many ways could they be arranged in the top two spots?

Ⓐ 6 ways
Ⓑ 2 ways
Ⓒ 3 ways
Ⓓ 8 ways

7. Sam is about to flip three coins. What is the probability he will flip all of the coins to heads?

Ⓐ 1 out of 4
Ⓑ 1 out of 6
Ⓒ 1 out of 8
Ⓓ 1 out of 2

8. Jona rolls one six-sided die and one four-sided die. What is the probability she will not roll a 2 or a 3 on either die?

Ⓐ 2 out of 3
Ⓑ 1 out of 3
Ⓒ 1 out of 4
Ⓓ 3 out of 4

9. Elsie rolled three four-sided dice. What is the probability she will roll one even and two odds?

Ⓐ 1 out of 3
Ⓑ 3 out of 8
Ⓒ 1 out of 4
Ⓓ 5 out of 8

10. What are the central tendencies of the following data set? (round to the nearest tenth)

{21, 21, 22, 23, 25, 27, 28, 31, 34, 34, 34, 37}

Ⓐ Mean: 28.1, Median: 27.5, Mode: 34
Ⓑ Mean: 28.5, Median: 26, Mode: none
Ⓒ Mean: 27.5, Median: 28, Mode: none
Ⓓ Mean: 27, Median: 27.5, Mode: none

11. **Are the events that make up the following compound events independent or dependent?**

Fill in the blanks by writing the correct type against each compound event.

Player chooses a game piece.	dependent / independent
Spin the spinner. Then spin again.	
Pick a colored marble from a jar. Pick another marble from the jar.	
Roll a dice. Then roll a dice again.	

12. **A jar is filled with 4 blue marbles, 2 yellow marbles, 5 red marbles, and 3 white marbles. Two marbles are chosen at random (one at a time) from the jar. What is the probability that a red marble and then a blue marble are chosen?**

Write the answer in the box. Reduce the fraction to its simplest form and write it in the box given below.

Chapter 6

Lesson 10: Represent Sample Spaces

You can scan the QR code given below or use the url to access additional EdSearch resources including videos and mobile apps related to *Represent Sample Spaces*.

ed Search *Represent Sample Spaces*

URL	QR Code
http://www.lumoslearning.com/a/7spc8b	

1. **If Robbie flips a quarter twice, what is the sample space for the possible outcomes?**

    Ⓐ HT, HH, TT, TH
    Ⓑ HT, TH
    Ⓒ HT, TT, TH
    Ⓓ HH, TT

2. **If Bret rolls a six-sided die twice, which table shows the sample space for possible outcomes?**

Ⓐ

	1	2	3	4	5	6
1	1, 1	1, 2	1, 3	1, 4	1, 5	1, 6
2	2, 1	2, 2	2, 3	2, 4	2, 5	2, 6
3	3, 1	3, 2	3, 3	3, 4	3, 5	3, 6
4	4, 1	4, 2	4, 3	4, 4	4, 5	4, 6
5	5, 1	5, 2	5, 3	5, 4	5, 5	5, 6
6	6, 1	6, 2	6, 3	6, 4	6, 5	6, 6

Ⓑ

	1	2	3	4	5	6
1	1, 1					
2		2, 2				
3			3, 3			
4				4, 4		
5					5, 5	
6						6, 6

Ⓒ

	1	2	3	4	5	6
1		1, 2	1, 3	1, 4	1, 5	1, 6
2	2, 1		2, 3	2, 4	2, 5	2, 6
3	3, 1	3, 2		3, 4	3, 5	3, 6
4	4, 1	4, 2	4, 3		4, 5	4, 6
5	5, 1	5, 2	5, 3	5, 4		5, 6
6	6, 1	6, 2	6, 3	6, 4	6, 5	

Ⓓ

	1	2	3	4
1	1, 1	1, 2	1, 3	1, 4
2	2, 1	2, 2	2, 3	2, 4
3	3, 1	3, 2	3, 3	3, 4
4	4, 1	4, 2	4, 3	4, 4
5	5, 1	5, 2	5, 3	5, 4
6	6, 1	6, 2	6, 3	6, 4

3. There are three colors of stones in a bag: red, green, and blue. Two stones are drawn out at random (one at a time). What are the possible outcomes in which exactly one blue stone might be drawn?

Ⓐ BR, GB BG
Ⓑ BG, BR, BB
Ⓒ RB, GB, BR, BG
Ⓓ BG, BR

4. A box contains both red checkers and black checkers. Four checkers are drawn out (one at a time). How many different possible outcomes would result in exactly three checkers being red?

Ⓐ 8
Ⓑ 2
Ⓒ 6
Ⓓ 4

5. A number between 1 and 10 (including 1 and 10) is chosen twice. How many different ways might the same number be chosen both times?

Ⓐ 5
Ⓑ 10
Ⓒ 0
Ⓓ 3

6. A number is chosen between 1 and 10 (including 1 and 10) twice. In how many different ways can you get an even number followed by a prime number?

Ⓐ 20
Ⓑ 9
Ⓒ 25
Ⓓ 12

7. Two six-side dice are rolled. How many different outcomes for the two dice would result in a total of 7 being rolled?

Ⓐ 10
Ⓑ 8
Ⓒ 6
Ⓓ 11

8. A stack of 20 cards are numbered 1 through 20. If cards are drawn from the stack until the 3 card is drawn, how many different outcomes would result in the 3 being drawn on the third draw?

   Ⓐ 37
   Ⓑ 112
   Ⓒ 20
   Ⓓ 342

9. A target has 4 rings on it. How many different ways might two arrows be distributed on the target?

   Ⓐ 4
   Ⓑ 16
   Ⓒ 8
   Ⓓ 7

10. If five different players have to be placed in five different positions on the team, how many different ways might this be done?

   Ⓐ 120
   Ⓑ 15
   Ⓒ 40
   Ⓓ 75

11. Every person attending the 11:00 movie put their ticket stub in a jar to enter a raffle. The theater owner selected 10 tickets and gave the winning people a prize. What is the sample in this situation? Circle the correct answer choice.

   Ⓐ Ticket Stubs
   Ⓑ 10 Winners
   Ⓒ Theater Owner
   Ⓓ People At The Movie

12. A bag contains red and blue marbles. In a representative sample of 10 marbles, there are 4 red marbles.

   Write the correct number of marbles into the blanks in the table.

	No. of Red Marbles	No. of Blue Marbles
If the bag has 100 marbles, estimate the number of red marbles and blue marbles in the bag.		
If the bag has 200 marbles, estimate the number of red marbles and blue marbles in the bag.		

Chapter 6

Lesson 11: Simulate Compound Events to Estimate Probability

You can scan the QR code given below or use the url to access additional EdSearch resources including videos and mobile apps related to *Simulate Compound Events to Estimate Probability*.

 **Simulate Compound Events to Estimate Probability**

URL	QR Code
http://www.lumoslearning.com/a/7spc8c	

1. **If 20% of applicants for a job are female, what is the probability that the first two applicants will be male?**

    (A) 64%
    (B) 80%
    (C) 60%
    (D) 52%

2. **If you want to simulate a random selection from a large population that is 40% adult and 60% children, how can you use slips of paper to do so?**

    (A) Make 5 slips of paper, 2 for adults and 3 for children. Randomly select slips of paper from the 5 to represent the choice of someone from the population.
    (B) Make 2 slips of paper, 1 for adults and 1 for children. Randomly select slips of paper from the 2 to represent the choice of someone from the population.
    (C) Make 100 slips of paper, 50 for adults and 50 for children. Randomly select slips of paper from the 100 to represent the choice of someone from the population.
    (D) Make 3 slips of paper, 1 for adults and 2 for children. Randomly select slips of paper from the 3 to represent the choice of someone from the population.

3. **A sandwich shop has 6 breads and 5 meats available for sandwiches. What is the probability that two people in a row will choose the same bread and meat combination?**

    (A) 1 out of 11
    (B) 1 out of 2
    (C) 1 out of 30
    (D) 1 out of 20

4. **A catalogue has sports uniforms for sale. There are 6 designs of shorts that can be combined with 4 designs of shirts. What is the probability that two teams choose different shorts and different shirts?**

    (A) 1 out of 2
    (B) 5 out of 8
    (C) 1 out of 4
    (D) 2 out of 7

5. **Sally has to choose a pair of pants and a pair of shoes to wear to her club meeting. She can't remember what she wore last time. She has 3 pairs of pants and 5 pairs of shoes to choose from. What is the probability that she will wear the same combination that she wore last time?**

    (A) 1 out of 15
    (B) 1 out of 8
    (C) 2 out of 11
    (D) 1 out of 125

6. Suppose that each of the next 5 days there is a 50% chance of rain. You want to know the likelihood of it not raining at all in those 5 days. How can you test that probability with a coin?

   Ⓐ Flip the coin. If it is heads, there will be no rain, and if it is tails, there will be rain. Flip it at least 10 times and see how many times no rain is the result.

   Ⓑ Flip a coin until you get tails, which will represent rain. If you get rain in fewer than 5 coin flips, it will rain in the next five days.

   Ⓒ Flip a coin five times in a row. Repeat this numerous times. Let heads represent no rain and tales represent rain. See how often the five coin flips result in no rain.

   Ⓓ Flip a coin five times. Take the number of times that tails is flipped, and divide it by five. That will tell you the probability of rain in the next five days.

7. Your lawnmower starts well four times out of five. If you have to mow the lawn three more times this season, what is the probability that it will start well all three times?

   Ⓐ About 51%
   Ⓑ About 43%
   Ⓒ About 87%
   Ⓓ About 22%

8. Evan works with his friend Luke. His friend is a good worker, but he has a tendency to be late to work too often. He only shows up on time about 50% of the time. He has already been late once in the first two days of the work week. What is the probability that he will be on time for the remaining three days of the workweek?

   Ⓐ 1 in 5
   Ⓑ 1 in 2
   Ⓒ 1 in 8
   Ⓓ 1 in 6

9. A group of three friends was curious about which day of the week each of them was born on. They decided to research it to find out. What is the probability that all three of them were born on the same day of the week?

   Ⓐ 1 out of 7
   Ⓑ 1 out of 49
   Ⓒ 1 out of 343
   Ⓓ 1 out of 21

10. Two friends both happened to buy new trucks from the same manufacturer in the same week. The manufacturer offers 4 models of trucks in 6 different colors. What is the probability that the two friends happened to buy the same model and color of truck?

   Ⓐ 1 out of 10
   Ⓑ 1 out of 14
   Ⓒ 1 out of 15
   Ⓓ 1 out of 24

11. A friend's family just welcomed their third child. It turns out that all 3 of the children in this family are girls, and they are not twins. Suppose that for each birth the probability of a "boy" birth is 0.5 and the probability of a "girl" birth is also 0.5. What are the chances of having three girls in the first 3 births?

   Write your answer in the box given below.

12. Suppose that for every birth of a baby the probability of a "boy" birth is 0.5 and the probability of a "girl" birth is also 0.5. Calculate the probabilities of having each of the situations described.

	0.125	0.375
Three boys	◯	◯
Two boys and a girl	◯	◯
Two girls and a boy	◯	◯
Three girls	◯	◯

End of Statistics and Probability

Notes

Additional Information

GMAS FAQs

What will GMAS Assessment Look Like?

In many ways, the GMAS assessments will be unlike anything many students have ever seen. The tests will be conducted online, requiring students complete tasks to assess a deeper understanding of the Georgia standards. The students will take the Summative Assessment at the end of the year.

The time for the Math Summative assessment for each grade is given below:

Estimated Time on Task in Minutes		
Grade	Section 1	Section 2
3	65	65
4	65	65
5	65	65
6	65	65
7	65	65
8	65	65

How is this Lumos tedBook aligned to GMAS Guidelines?

The practice tests provided in the Lumos Program were created to reflect the depth and rigor of the GMAS assessments based on the information published by the test administrator. However, the content and format of the GMAS assessment that is officially administered to the students could be different compared to these practice tests. You can get more information about this test by visiting https://www.gadoe.org/Curriculum-Instruction-and-Assessment/Assessment/Pages/EOG-Study-Resource-Guides.aspx

What item types are included in the Online GMAS Test?

Because the assessment is online, the test will consist of a combination of new types of questions:

1. Selected Response or Multiple choice questions
2. Multi select or two part questions
3. Drag and Drop
4. Hot text
5. Equation editor
6. Plot the point
7. Bar chart

For more information on 2021-22 Assessment year, visit
http://www.lumoslearning.com/a/gmas-2021-faqs
OR Scan the **QR Code**

Discover Engaging and Relevant Learning Resources

Lumos EdSearch is a safe search engine specifically designed for teachers and students. Using EdSearch, you can easily find thousands of standards-aligned learning resources such as questions, videos, lessons, worksheets and apps. Teachers can use EdSearch to create custom resource kits to perfectly match their lesson objective and assign them to one or more students in their classroom.

To access the EdSearch tool, use the search box after you log into Lumos StepUp or use the link provided below.

http://www.lumoslearning.com/a/edsearchb	

The Lumos Standards Coherence map provides information about previous level, next level and related standards. It helps educators and students visually explore learning standards. It's an effective tool to help students progress through the learning objectives. Teachers can use this tool to develop their own pacing charts and lesson plans. Educators can also use the coherence map to get deep insights into why a student is struggling in a specific learning objective.

Teachers can access the Coherence maps after logging into the StepUp Teacher Portal or use the link provided below.

http://www.lumoslearning.com/a/coherence-map	

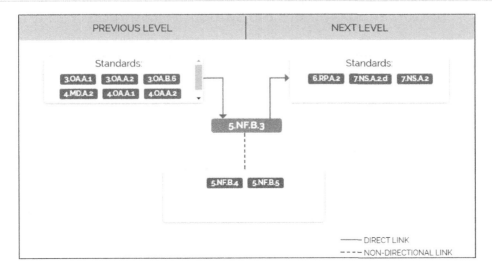

What if I buy more than one Lumos Study Program?

Step 1

Visit the URL and login to your account.
http://www.lumoslearning.com

Step 2

Click on 'My tedBooks' under the "Account" tab.
Place the Book Access Code and submit.

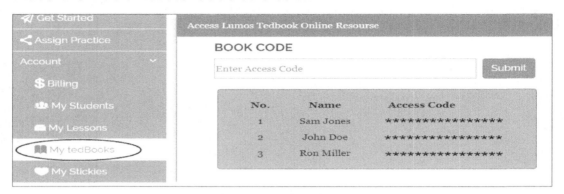

Step 3

To add the new book for a registered student, choose the
○ Existing Student button and select the student and submit.

Assign To ⊙

○ Existing Student   ○ Add New student

○ Sam Jones

○ John Doe

○ Ron Miller

Submit

To add the new book for a new student, choose the ○ Add New student
button and complete the student registration.

Assign To ⊙

○ Existing Student   ● Add New student

Register Your TedBook

Student Name: Enter First Name   Enter Last Name

Student Login*

Password*

Submit

Lumos StepUp® Mobile App FAQ For Students

What is the Lumos StepUp® App?

It is a FREE application you can download onto your Android Smartphones, tablets, iPhones, and iPads.

What are the Benefits of the StepUp® App?

This mobile application gives convenient access to Practice Tests, Common Core State Standards, Online Workbooks, and learning resources through your Smartphone and tablet computers.

- Fourteen Technology enhanced question types in both MATH and ELA
- Sample questions for Arithmetic drills
- Standard specific sample questions
- Instant access to the Common Core State Standards

Do I Need the StepUp® App to Access Online Workbooks?

No, you can access Lumos StepUp® Online Workbooks through a personal computer. The StepUp® app simply enhances your learning experience and allows you to conveniently access StepUp® Online Workbooks and additional resources through your smartphone or tablet.

How can I Download the App?

Visit **lumoslearning.com/a/stepup-app** using your Smartphone or tablet and follow the instructions to download the app.

QR Code
for Smartphone
Or Tablet Users

Lumos StepUp® Mobile App FAQ For Parents and Teachers

What is the Lumos StepUp® App?

It is a free app that teachers can use to easily access real-time student activity information as well as assign learning resources to students. Parents can also use it to easily access school-related information such as homework assigned by teachers and PTA meetings. It can be downloaded onto smartphones and tablets from popular App Stores.

What are the Benefits of the Lumos StepUp® App?

It provides convenient access to

- Standards aligned learning resources for your students
- An easy to use Dashboard
- Student progress reports
- Active and inactive students in your classroom
- Professional development information
- Educational Blogs

How can I Download the App?

Visit **lumoslearning.com/a/stepup-app** using your Smartphone or tablet and follow the instructions to download the app.

**QR Code
for Smartphone
Or Tablet Users**

Progress Chart

Standard		Lesson	Page No.	Practice		Mastered	Re-practice /Reteach
GMAS	CCSS			Date	Score		
MGSE7.RP.1	7.RP.A.1	Unit Rates	10				
MGSE7.RP.2a	7.RP.A.2.A	Understanding and Representing Proportions	14				
MGSE7.RP.2b	7.RP.A.2.B	Finding Constant of Proportionality	19				
MGSE7.RP.2c	7.RP.A.2.C	Represent Proportions by Equations	24				
MGSE7.RP.2d	7.RP.A.2.D	Significance of Points on Graphs of Proportions	29				
MGSE7.RP.3	7.RP.A.3	Applying Ratios and Percents	37				
MGSE7.NS.1	7.NS.A.1	Rational Numbers, Addition & Subtraction	41				
MGSE7.NS.1b	7.NS.A.1.B	Add and Subtract Rational Numbers	46				
MGSE7.NS.1c	7.NS.A.1.C	Additive Inverse and Distance Between Two Points on a Number Line	51				
MGSE7.NS.1d	7.NS.A.1.D	Strategies for Adding and Subtracting Rational Numbers	56				
MGSE7.NS.2	7.NS.A.2	Rational Numbers, Multiplication and Division	60				
MGSE7.NS.2b	7.NS.A.2.B	Rational Numbers as Quotients of Integers	65				
MGSE7.NS.2c	7.NS.A.2.C	Strategies for Multiplying and Dividing Rational Numbers	70				

Standard		Lesson	Page No.	Practice		Mastered	Re-practice /Reteach
GMAS	CCSS			Date	Score		
MGSE7.NS.2d	7.NS.A.2.D	Converting Between Rational Numbers and Decimals	75				
MGSE7.NS.3	7.NS.A.3	Solving Real World Problems	79				
MGSE7.EE.1	7.EE.A.1	Applying Properties to Rational Expressions	83				
MGSE7.EE.2	7.EE.A.2	Interpreting the Meanings of Expressions	89				
MGSE7.EE.4	7.EE.B.4	Modeling Using Equations or Inequalities	95				
MGSE7.EE.3	7.EE.B.3	Solving Multi-Step Problems	99				
MGSE7.EE.4b	7.EE.B.4.B	Linear Inequality Word Problems	103				
MGSE7.G.1	7.G.A.1	Scale Models	108				
MGSE7.G.2	7.G.A.2	Drawing Plane (2-D) Figures	114				
MGSE7.G.3	7.G.A.3	Cross Sections of 3-D Figures	119				
MGSE7.G.4	7.G.B.4	Circles	124				
MGSE7.G.5	7.G.B.5	Angles	128				
MGSE7.G.6	7.G.B.6	Finding Area, Volume, & Surface Area	133				
MGSE7.SP.1	7.SP.A.1	Sampling a Population	139				
MGSE7.SP.2	7.SP.A.2	Describing Multiple Samples	144				
MGSE7.SP.3	7.SP.B.3	Mean, Median, and Mean Absolute Deviation	151				

Standard		Lesson	Page No.	Practice		Mastered	Re-practice /Reteach
GMAS	CCSS			Date	Score		
MGSE7.SP.4	7.SP.B.4	Mean, Median, and Mode	158				
MGSE7.SP.5	7.SP.C.5	Understanding Probability	164				
MGSE7.SP.6	7.SP.C.6	Predicting Using Probability	169				
MGSE7.SP.7a	7.SP.C.7.A	Using Probability Models	174				
MGSE7.SP.7b	7.SP.C.7.B	Probability Models from Observed Frequencies	178				
MGSE7.SP.7b	7.SP.C.7.B	Find the Probability of a Compound Event	182				
MGSE7.SP.8b	7.SP.C.8.B	Represent Sample Spaces	187				
MGSE7.SP.8c	7.SP.C.8.C	Simulate Compound Events to Estimate Probability	191				

Lumos Learning
Developed by Expert Teachers

Grade **7**

GEORGIA
ENGLISH
LANGUAGE ARTS LITERACY
GMAS Practice

Student Copy

Updated for 2021-22

ONLINE

2 GMAS Practice Tests

7 Question Types

Georgia Department of Education does not sponsor or endorse this product.

Available

- At Leading book stores
- Online www.LumosLearning.com

Made in the USA
Middletown, DE
11 March 2022

62364543R00117